D1300802

Presented To:

RANDY

From:

Date:

1/1/17

THE SOUL SURVIVOR

THE SOUL

THE

SURVIVOR

CAPTAIN JOE TOWNSEND

SHAWN DOYLE

DESTINY IMAGE® PUBLISHERS, INC.

P.O. Box 310, Shippensburg, PA 17257-0310

"Promoting Inspired Lives"

This book and all other Destiny Image, Revival Press, MercyPlace, Fresh Bread, Destiny Image Fiction, and Treasure House books are available at Christian bookstores and distributors worldwide.

For a U.S. bookstore nearest you, call **1-800-722-6774.**

For more information on foreign distributors, call **717-532-3040.**

Reach us on the Internet: **www.destinyimage.com.**

13 DIGIT ISBN: 978-0-7684-3958-8

E-Book ISBN: 978-0-7684-8938-5

For Worldwide Distribution, Printed in the U.S.A.

1 2 3 4 5 6 7 8 / 14 13 12 11

Dedication

To Kelley, Laura Lee, and Tara Nicole, I love and miss you every day of my life.

To Carol, Dave, and Lisa—thank you for being my second chance at having a great family.

—Joe

To Cindy, my wife and CEO (Chief Encouragement Officer), thanks for just being you.

—Shawn

Acknowledgments

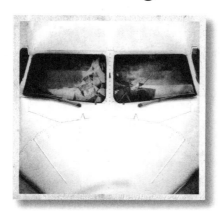

This has been a fantastic life for me, in which I have been blessed with many great friends and associates who are too numerous to mention each by name. You have all been valued as an important part of my life, even if we had only a brief time together. There have been times on the mountain tops of life, but many valleys as well. It was your friendships that soared me over the tops and also lifted me out of the valleys.

My first acknowledgment goes to my co-author and friend, Shawn Doyle, for his hard work in writing this book. You have had your share of adversity in your own life, and together we are able to share our trials with so many others who face adversity in their lives. It is my hope that this story gives the readers confidence that they can overcome any obstacle.

A special thank you goes to my family for being there for me. My parents, Al and Betty (who are now in eternity) were the glue to keep us together. Thank you to my sister Rose, along with her husband, Shawn, for moving into my home with me after my hospital adventure. Thank you to my sister Mary Anne for accompanying my father to Albany the day after the accident and, with her medical wisdom, becoming my advocate. Thank you to my sister Elizabeth for many fine meals and hair cuts on the patio. Thank you to my brother, Father George, for his strength and his many sincere prayers for me. Thank you to Sister Margaret, who flew in to visit and comfort me. Thank you to Roger Singleton for marrying my sister!

There are many medical professionals who put me back together. Dr. Jay Trabin got me transferred from Albany to St. Mary's Hospital in West Palm Beach. Dr. Frank Cook was there when I arrived to care for my many orthopedic injuries. Dr. James Clancy performed reconstructive surgeries on my feet and helped put all of the medical terminology in my records into layman terms. Thank you also to the many surgeons, nurses, and staff in Albany, Georgia, at Phoebe-Putney Hospital who put my broken body back together.

Thank you to the Fitzgerald Georgia Fire and Rescue men and women who were there to pull me out of the airplane and tend to my three angels, Kelley, Laura Lee, and Tara Nicole. Thank you also to the medical staff at the Fitzgerald Dorminy Medical Center for the initial care for me and my girls. Thank you to Danny Boy Lewis who arranged with my insurance carrier to fly me to West Palm Beach on a private medical jet.

I only have space to list a few of my pilot friends, although there are many more who have been there for me. Thank you to First Officer and close friend, Barry Van Wagner, who escorted my Three Angels on their final flight home. Thank you to all my good buddies, Captain Joe Piazza, Captain James Ray, Second Officer Dexter Franklin, Captain Conrad Groh, Captain Roy Paget, Captain Steve Boswell, Captain Dean Brisson, and Captain Don Gieseke, along with the Pilots For Christ group and

Captain Don Moore of the pilot's union bereavement who counseled my family.

Thank you to my physical therapist, Kevin Kunkel, who pushed me to walk unencumbered from walkers and canes.

Thank you to all of the US Airways employees who have been helpful in my travels, especially Agent Kathy Sitchko, who came to visit and take me to lunch.

There are very many great friends about whom I could write a full book to thank them for their part of my life. You are definitely counted in my heart and mind.

Thank you, J.D. DeBoskey, for helping me to arrange the best marriage proposal ever.

Thank you, Nurse Tara from Albany, for your love and kindness.

Thank you, Gloria Tanner, for your love and kindness and for writing me a heartfelt poem.

Thank you to my many SSR FANATIC friends, especially "Big Wave" Duane Morgan for all of the photography expertise for this book

Thank you to my many friends in my former neighborhood, Banyan Lakes, who were there for my emotional support, as well as feeding me when I was hungry.

To Kelley's family, I wish this story had a different ending.

To my church families at St. Peter's United Methodist Church in Wellington, Florida, and the Seventh Day Adventist Church in Littleton, Colorado. Thank you Pastors Rainer Richter and Bruce Aalborg for your spiritual guidance. Thank you also to all of my church friends who have been and continue to be an important part of my life.

The greatest acknowledgment is to my wife, Carol, who is always there for me. She is not only my wife, but is my best friend. Thank you, Carol, for all of your help in my everyday life as well as your help in writing this book. Your devotion to me and your children is truly admirable, and that is why I love you so much.

—Joe Townsend

To Alexis Gastwirth, many thanks for your research and help and for creating a rocking Website.

To Joe Townsend, for having the courage and the heart to tell his story. I am honored to call you my friend.

To the fine editors at Destiny Image for their great work—Christina and Amy.

To Wilmer and Nathan for believing in this project from day one.

—Shawn Doyle

Contents

Chapter 1

The Day We Fell to Earth

The bad news is time flies. The good news is you are the pilot.
—Michael Altshuler[1]

It was a beautiful, sunny fall afternoon. I could almost smell the crisp leaves in the light, cool wind breezing in from Canada. I walked on to yet another plane to fly to West Palm Beach. My name is Shawn Doyle, and I am a road warrior. I travel so frequently that I am often upgraded to first class. Traveling first class has its advantages, and I have met some really interesting people in the seats next to me.

On this particular flight, the man sitting in the inside seat next to me boarded after I did. As he approached, he pointed to his seat and said, "Hello there. Sorry to bother you. I am sitting in that seat." He smiled warmly. I stood up and moved so he could slide in. He was tall and thin with brown hair that turned slightly gray at the temples.

Ladies and gentlemen, our plane is pretty full. As people are getting on this afternoon's flight, please put your largest bags up above and the smaller bags underneath the seat in front of you...

"Hey there. I'm Joe Townsend. Nice to meet you," he said it in a quiet, soft voice while flashing me a thousand-watt smile. He shook my hand firmly. I realized he had a way about him that I can't describe exactly—a quality, a warmth, a spark. Some would call it personality or likeability. The French would call it *je ne sais quoi*, which literally means, "I don't know." Joe had an indescribable quality about him that I couldn't quite put my finger on, but it made me want to be friends with him.

"Nice to meet you, Joe. I'm Shawn Doyle."

We both settled back in our seats and waited for the pre-flight announcements to end so that we could take off. As soon as we were cleared for takeoff, the plane roared smoothly down the runway, lifted into the sky, and headed south into the sunset.

"So, Joe, where are you headed today?" I asked.

"I am headed to my home in West Palm Beach," he replied.

I paused, processing this information. "So do you live there?"

"Well," he said, "I have a home in West Palm and a home in Littleton, Colorado."

"Nice."

"Where are you headed?" he asked.

"I am headed down to West Palm on business," I explained.

"What do you do, Shawn?" he asked.

"I am a professional speaker, trainer, and consultant," I replied.

"Wow! Really? On what topics?" he asked.

"Well, I talk about a lot of things, but mostly leadership, motivation, and creativity," I said.

His eyes lit up. He smiled. "Well, that is really neat. I kind of always enjoyed that stuff. I took a Dale Carnegie course on speaking when I was 20 years old. That is really cool. So a speaker, huh? Wow. So do you have any books out?"

"Yeah, I have a few."

"Wow. That is super cool."

I asked him what he did for a living. He paused in the funny way that people pause when they are searching for the right answer. Maybe he had the answer, but paused because he didn't know how I was going to react to it; I am not really sure. For a moment, his eyes kind of had a cloudy look. He paused and said, "Well, I am a medically retired US Airways pilot. I am out on long-term disability because I was in an accident."

There are times when the arc of your life changes dramatically and in a heartbeat. The thing is that you often don't recognize it at the time. Joe and I didn't know that this was a defining moment for both of us.

I try to be aware of the feelings of people around me, although I will admit I don't always succeed. I sat there for a few minutes in deep thought and wondered if I should ask Joe what happened. I had a conversation with myself in my mind.

> If I ask, it might be perceived as being rude or pushy or insensitive.

> But, on the other hand, if I don't ask him, maybe that would appear as if I didn't really care.

> He brought it up, so maybe he wants to talk about it.

So I decided to take the risk, however small it seems now.

"Wow. Joe, I am sorry to hear you were in an accident. I uhhh…well, do you mind me asking you what happened? I mean, if you don't want to talk about it, please don't…if it will make you uncomfortable in any way."

He looked at me with an expression I couldn't read exactly. I thought it might have been a look of sadness, peace, or even sincerity. He looked me straight in the eye, and shifted slightly in his seat. He said quietly, "No, it's OK. It's a story I would like to tell if you want to hear it."

I smiled at Joe, put my seat back, and folded my arms across my chest, "Well, I don't exactly have anywhere to go in the next few hours. Fire away, Mr. Joe Townsend."

So I heard Joe's amazing and true story.

I have always loved to fly and have flown all my life; I was just flat-out born to fly. I was a professional airline pilot. I flew as a captain on the MD Super 80, nicknamed the Mad Dog. Before getting hired with Piedmont Airlines, now US Airways, I flew corporate and charter jets out of West Palm Beach, Florida. My piloting experience is in excess of 12,000 flight hours. That equates to over 500 days, 24 hours a day, behind the control wheel. That's a lot of airplane food to digest!

For several years, I had my own Bellanca Citabria, a tandem seated plane with the pilot's seat in front. Now that was a cool plane! I became proficient at flying upside down and inside out. I used to get a kick out of taking friends up with me, but I made sure they had a sick sack so their lunch would not end up on the back of my neck. One friend did have to use the sick sack so it did come in handy to have them available.

My friend Bob Bentz lent me his plane—a white, blue striped, four-seater, Bellanca Turbo Viking—for a trip to my wife Kelley's cousin's beautiful farm in Fitzgerald, Georgia, over Thanksgiving weekend in 1996. It was a beautiful plane. Bob had flown his family in the airplane to Venice, Florida, to have lunch the week before. For some strange reason, Bob had difficulty getting full power on the plane for the return flight to West Palm Beach. As a result, they left the plane in Venice and rented a car and drove home.

The mechanics in Venice made the repairs, so my girls and I drove the rental car back to Venice the following week for the flight to Georgia. After a preflight inspection, I took it for a test flight and everything on the plane performed normally. Like many pilots, I was always a big one on safety. I would never put my girls in an unsafe plane. We pilots are kind of funny that way when it comes to safety, because we know that you don't get a second chance. The plane flew normally to Georgia; we had full power for the flight and the plane operated well. The weather and conditions were perfect: blue skies.

We had a great time being around family and friends. We all cooked and ate until our bellies were busting. Isn't that what everyone does at Thanksgiving? All of the kids, my girls and their cousins, played and ran around the cabin. They enjoyed being in a kid's paradise—a farm with animals, hay, barns, and cotton fields. We roasted marshmallows at night around the fire. Tara, our toddler, was only 18 months old, so she was excited about everything that weekend. The girls had been able to see a ten-day-old calf, and they loved petting its soft muzzle. Laura was excited because she got to pick raw cotton and had stuffed her cute little blue-jean pockets with it to show to her friends during show-and-tell at school. It was, in every sense, the perfect long weekend.

Every time I came back on the four-wheeler from a morning of hunting on the farm, which consisted of sitting in a tree-stand waiting for some unsuspecting deer to walk by, Laura came running up ready for a ride. In her sweet, young voice, she merrily cried out, "Daddy, Daddy, will you please take me for a ride?" Sometimes I would even load Kelley, Laura, and Tara on and take a family ride around the farm. There was a trail along the edge of the woods that went by "the bone pile," an area where they laid the cows to rest after they had died. That fascinated the girls.

It was a snappy, fall morning on December 1st, 1996, when I got into the van with Kelley, my wife, and my two little angels, Laura Lee and Tara Nicole. We were headed for the local airport. We had just spent a wonderful, fun-filled Thanksgiving weekend on the farm.

The girls were wearing matching sundresses made of bright orange-yellow and white fabric. I don't know where they got them, but my wife Kelley had a dress in matching fabric. Laura Lee, the four-year-old, was a beautiful blond with blue eyes, and Tara was her sister's opposite, with brown hair and brown eyes. Laura resembled Kelley when she was that age, and Tara was the spitting image of me, except that she was a much prettier child.

Before leaving the cabin, we ate a quick breakfast, as there were tons of great leftover desserts to fatten our bellies. We headed to the airport to fly home to Florida. The girls were excited; they always loved to fly. I guess the apple doesn't fall far from the tree.

So I got the plane ready by completing my preflight inspection with draining the two wing fuel sumps, checking topped off fuel tanks, draining the engine fuel sump, and checking the oil level. I was very focused on getting everything prepared. I hopped into the cockpit to arrange my aeronautical charts, checking out my flight plan as the girls put in their bags and got settled in. The girls were laughing and giggling and full of energy. I was a little concerned about the weather—there was a dark gray cold front coming in from the northwest. It looked like a moody Andrew Wyeth painting, a blue-gray wash slashing across the sky with jutting, muscular clouds. The south was clear with bright, Renoir-blue skies all the way to Florida. We were headed south toward Florida, and I knew that we could be off the ground and on our way before the weather arrived.

Tara, our 18-month-old toddler, sat in a car seat in the back of the plane with Kelley. Kelley, being a typical mom, liked to be back there in case Tara needed her. Laura sat proudly in the passenger seat beside me. She liked being my copilot and liked the view from the front. It's funny, but Laura was always the daredevil anyway. Laura loved to walk along the second-level railing of the back deck of our house while I held her hand, and she balanced like a skilled gymnast on a balance beam. She was never afraid.

We took off from the Fitzgerald Airport and lifted off the runway with ease as I had done hundreds, no, many thousands of times before. How routine is takeoff in a small plane? When I had done it so many times before, it was as routine as brushing my teeth. I had it down.

Very quickly into the flight, I began to lose power and I decided to turn back to the airport in Fitzgerald. It was a decision that would change my life and the lives of others, forever.

I am sure you have heard the story of Captain Sully on the famous US Airways flight 1549. Captain Sully had to decide in a heartbeat whether he would attempt to make it to Teterboro, New Jersey, or try to land in the Hudson River. As you know, he chose the Hudson. To this day, I wish I would have landed on a highway, or in a peanut field, but I turned the plane around to return to the airport, as I believed I had enough altitude to make it to the runway.

Even at full throttle, which is like pressing the accelerator pedal of your car all the way to the floorboard, the plane was dramatically losing power and dangerously losing altitude at a rapid pace. I was lined up to land on Runway 1, which is 5,000 feet long and paved. There was a runway-approach lighting tower sticking up in my path, as I was getting closer to the airport. The throttle was full forward, and I was trying to get as much power out of the engine as I could. The engine was coughing and backfiring violently while we continued losing altitude. I tried to squeak out enough altitude by pulling back hard on the yoke to clear the approach tower.

The limited airspeed allowed two choices: either fly into the tower or hope I had enough airspeed to fly over it. Flying into the light tower would, of course, have been suicidal. I did not have a death wish nor was I a kamikaze pilot. The plane made it over the light tower by inches, but there was not enough airspeed and the nose dropped. There was no more lift, and I thought to myself, *OH-MY- GOD-THIS-ISN'T-HAPPENING!* as we crashed nose-first into the ground with incredible, violent force. The plane landed with an explosion of noise: metal crashed against metal and into unforgiving soil.

Originally, I thought I had enough altitude to make it to the runway. What I could not have known was that the spark plugs were fouling out or failing rapidly. Once I decided to land the sick aircraft on the runway, instead of in a field, my flight path was committed to that approach, especially because we were flying at a low altitude. The approach speed of the Viking is 80 knots or 92 MPH, and the stall speed is 61 knots or 70 MPH. If the airspeed falls below the stall speed, the nose always drops, as there is not enough airflow over the wings to sustain lift. When passing over the approach light tower, I would have had to be flying at about 40 feet above the ground to clear the tower without hitting it. That would have been where the stall occurred, as I would have pulled back on the controls in my attempt to clear it. With the wings stalling at 40 feet, and the nose dropping, there was not enough altitude to recover from the stall, especially when I already had the throttles full forward to maximize the available power.

You can imagine what kind of damage would be done when you hit a hard object at 70 MPH and drop from 40 feet above the ground.

The massive force of the crash caused the nose of the plane to split apart in a violent explosion of metal and glass. Fortunately, there was no fire, which would have been expected because the fuel tanks were full. I almost made it. I crash-landed 300 yards from the runway in a dusty little airport in Georgia. Three hundred yards! We were only three football fields from landing safely on the runway pavement and well beyond the approach light towers!

Now, I must tell you that all this stuff I'm telling you about the crash is not from my own memory. I have no memory of the crash. Thank God! From the time we took off, I remember nothing—it is a blank, white space for me. My head hit the artificial horizon indicator knob, which broke through my skull, causing a severe brain injury and preventing me from remembering anything from the crash. This knob is also known as the attitude indicator adjustor. The ADI, Attitude Direction Indicator, most definitely had a bad attitude that day!

The severe nature of my injury also blinded me temporarily. I thank God to this day that I lost my sight, otherwise I would have seen the death of my little angels. It would have been a terrible sight. I didn't want to have that terrible memory. My wife Kelley was found lifeless, shielding little Tara. She was hugging Tara's body to protect her. That was so typical of her as a mom. Tara Nicole was taken to a local hospital, and then to a trauma center, Phoebe Putney in Albany. They could not save her, due to the severe head trauma, and her little heart just stopped. Laura Lee was gone as well—she died on impact. So that day, I lost my entire family—they all went to Heaven at once. In the blink of an eye, my life, as I knew it, changed forever and ever.

Excerpt from the National Transportation Safety Board Report

Injuries: 3 Fatal, 1 Serious

The pilot could not recall the accident flight and there were no impact witnesses. He stated that it was misting rain during loading and the engine run up. He also noted a weather front moving in from the north and clear in the

Southeast. Relatives helped load the plane and watched it depart then drove to Florida. After an unknown elapsed time an ear witness heard fluctuating engine sounds followed by an impact. He found the plane south of runway 19. The airplane had impacted in a steep left wing and nose down attitude. Subsequent investigation revealed the air intake box alternate air door had broken loose. A fresh fracture was evident in the door hinge. The spark plugs were sooted. The fuel injection system was tested within limits.

The NTSB determines the probable causes of this accident as follows:

A loss of engine power due to the blockage of the intake manifold of the induction air system, by the broken alternate air door, and the loss of aircraft control for undetermined reasons.

Ladies and gentlemen we will be starting cabin service now....

"Well, I think I'm gonna run to the big boys room," Joe said. He stood up and wobbled a little. "When I sit too long, I get a little stiff." He stretched and walked a bit stiff-legged to the bathroom.

"Okey Dokey," I said.

I sat quietly thinking about Joe's story. I was lost in thought. *Good God in Heaven. How does someone experience this and move on? I mean the whole family in one day? Gone?* I have a wife and a daughter, and I couldn't imagine them being gone in a moment's notice. I wondered how I would feel if I lost my entire family. In one day. Gone. I fought back the lump in my throat and the tears in my eyes. I didn't want Joe to see that when he came back. Plus, I realized that he had lost his livelihood on top of that. Wow. I had a feeling similar to the one I had after I visited the Oklahoma City bombing memorial site. I was sad and grateful for the blessed life I have. I am so fortunate.

I thought of the poem President Ronald Reagan mentioned at the funeral for the Challenger Shuttle astronauts.

Oh! I have slipped the surly bond of Earth

And danced the skies on laughter-silvered wings;

Sunward I've climbed, and joined the tumbling mirth...[2]

I was feeling...how was I feeling? Lucky. I was feeling fortunate. Grateful. I *have* a wife, and I *have* a daughter. Yes, OK, we all have trials and tribulations, but what this man has experienced no one should really ever have to. It has no comparison. What we whine and complain about is meaningless and trivial, small potatoes, nothing. We are "sweating the small stuff." We are really ungrateful.

"Hidey Ho! I'm back," Joe said with a glowing grin on his face.

"Oh. Hey there, Joe. Doing all right?"

"It was good to stretch." He sighed and smiled.

"Yup. I always say nothing better than a good stretch," I said, still lost in thought.

"Well, Joe, I have to say your story is very touching, and sad, and amazing. I really appreciate you sharing it with me. But, Joe...I just have to ask—and I hope I am not stepping over the line here—but, how do you overcome something like that? I mean you had physical injuries and then the grief..." I shook my head and sat back in my seat, letting out air.

"Yes, the toughest part was not the injury, or the accident, or the loss. It was...well, learning to live with it. Suicide would have been the easy way out, but that's not me. *Quitting is not in my makeup.* I have always had a can-do attitude. I have never been a quitter. They say that God never gives you more than you can handle. God must have thought I was Superman, Batman, and Spiderman all in one, because I was given a "shipload" to handle," he said, chuckling at his humor.

"So what happened to you after the crash?"

"You really want to know the whole story?"

"Yes, I do, Joe. If you don't mind telling it, I would be honored to listen."

"Well, it's pretty intense, but here goes…"

When the plane struck the ground with violent force, the front firewall split and separated from the aircraft. My ankles also split apart, leaving my feet dangling by the skin along the outer edge of my feet. My left leg was broken in three places, and both of my kneecaps were broken. I had internal injuries in my abdomen where the yoke hit me with tremendous force. My right arm was cut badly as I tried to protect Laura from the impact. I still have scars on my hand where I reached out to protect her.

A crop-duster pilot, James Clark, was first on the scene. He lived nearby. Dressed in a blue work shirt and dusty jeans, he got down and leaned into the wreckage. He asked, "Are you OK in there?" I replied, "Lord, help me!" three times. He wasn't able to see into the plane wreckage much, and it had started raining. He asked if anyone was with me. I said, "No, I am alone!"

Ironically, I wasn't alone, but said I was. Isn't that kind of odd? The severe head trauma had confused my short-term memory. I had been blinded by my brain injury and couldn't see. I was pinned into the wreckage. James then told me he was going to get help.

The fire crew had to use the Jaws of Life to cut open the front of the plane, so they could drag me out through the windshield, which they had to break to extract me. My feet were barely hanging onto my legs and they wrapped them up. The strange thing is that I was conscious and blind, but I have no memory of that time period at all. None. I guess in a way it was a form of protection. One poor young paramedic actually lost his lunch when he saw the horrific scene of our crash and injuries. I guess the scene was just a nightmare to see. Firemen and paramedics not directly involved were standing off to the side praying for us in the light misty rain. When I got into the ambulance, I told them it was dark in there.

So, in my first baby step back to life, I made it to the hospital alive, but my fight had just begun.

My prognosis at the Phoebe Putney Hospital in Albany was grim, as they all thought they were going to lose me. No one on the staff thought I would actually make it. No one noticed it at the time, but I was taken to room 6, which many people called the "miracle room." Fifteen pints of blood were transfused into me because of all of my blood loss.

Then, in the first few hours I was in the ICU, I went into cardiac arrest, because a huge blood clot had formed around my heart from the transfused blood. For the next 45 minutes, they worked furiously to get my heart started and to get me stable again. When my heart stopped, I had a stroke, and then went into a coma. The surgeons thought I wouldn't survive the next few days. I refused to die.

I had 11 hours of surgery where doctors rebuilt my kneecaps and reattached my severed ankles. They put plates, rods, and screws in my legs, ankles, and feet. A neurosurgeon was patching the hole in my forehead, and other surgeons were slicing out six inches of my intestines.

It is really hard to say, but I didn't get to attend the funeral of my angels. They didn't think I was going to make it. That still bothers me.

While I was in a coma in Georgia, my very good friend, Barry Van Wagner, flew to Atlanta to escort the coffins on US Airways back to West Palm Beach. That must have been really hard for him. He has a heart of gold. I will always be grateful for what he did.

The funeral was held at St. Peters United Methodist Church, and more than 700 people packed the church to sing hymns and to also pray for me back in Albany. The Reverend Rainer Richter at the funeral said Kelley and the girls blessed everyone they knew. He also said that life brings things people have no control over, and urged people not to second guess themselves or be angry with God.

Barry later told me that when he arrived in Charlotte with the coffins to make the connection to West Palm Beach, he was greeted by half a dozen of my fellow comrades dressed in their dapper pilot uniforms and caps. The Chief Pilot organized the ceremonial off-loading and reloading onto the next airplane. Barry said that it was like a Military Honor Guard maneuver that moved him to tears. Barry was not only a very good friend of mine, but had also known Kelley since their childhood. It is moving and heart-warming to know that my friends were out there on the ramp in the early, cool night hours, blessing my girls with respect.

Over 700 family and friends attended the funeral. The procession to the cemetery was several hundred cars long. A local reporter, Paul Owers, saw the procession and thought a local distinguished politician had died because it was so long. He was amazed when he learned it was for two little girls and their mom. I think that says a lot about my wife and our girls.

EXCERPT FROM *THE PALM BEACH POST*

The line to see Kelley and the girls at the wake stretched outside Quattlebaum-Holleman-Burse Funeral Home down Olive Avenue in West Palm Beach. Some of Joe and Kelley's friends said they had waited three hours. Others waited too but had to leave before making it inside.

It was a testament to the kind of person Kelley was. Classmates at Palm Beach Community College called her "Mom" even back then because she watched out for them. She was responsible, often making sure friends didn't drive if they'd had too much to drink.

Many of Joe's friends and pilots from all areas of the country flew in for the funeral and wore their dapper pilot uniforms in respect to their friendship. Joe also had many friends from the numerous activities and hobbies that he participated in.

After 11:00 pm, with the line still snaking around the block, the funeral directors politely asked Kelley's parents if it was Ok to call it a night.

They said it was.

The sight of three white caskets, two of them just tiny boxes jolted the people who jammed St Peters United Methodist Church the next day.

The funeral was officiated by a Greek Orthodox priest, a Catholic priest and a Methodist Minister. Kelley's family say it is fitting that Kelley, who saw both sides of any argument, could bring together three different religions under one roof. The Catholic priest, Father Julian Harris, softly explained that Kelley's younger daughter, 18 month old Tara, would be least afraid of heaven because she had been there most recently. He went on to say that she and 4 year old Laura Lee would take mommy by the hand and lead her into heaven so she wouldn't be frightened. Rev. Rainer Richter officiated as he was the pastor of the church with many moving words also.

When the prayers were being said at the graveside, to the astonishment of many, a triple rainbow appeared in the sky. I know that sounds like a corny movie, but it really happened. I wish I had been there to see it. That must have really been something to see.

When I woke up from my coma, ten days after the accident, I was stiff and sore, and I felt the burns from where the shock paddles had been used to revive me several times. A nurse walked into the room and I asked her weakly, in my slow, slurred speech, "Nurse? Where are my wife and kids?" She turned and said quietly, "They are with God in Heaven." I felt as if my blood had been injected with antifreeze.

No, no, no, no, no, no, that couldn't possibly be true! She was surely mistaken. I was groggy, and I fell back to sleep. The very next morning—the worst morning of all mornings of my life—I got the news from my father and my sister Mary Anne. It was so hard for them to look me in the eye and tell me: the girls were all in Heaven just like the nurse had said. It was true, and it broke my heart into a million pieces. I had been blind, asleep, and never knew any of it. Everyone else knew but me. I was asleep and woke up to a nightmare. It was different though because you can wake up from a nightmare.

Ladies and gentlemen, we are now preparing the cabin for our landing in West Palm Beach, so please turn off all electronic devices...

"Joe, I really appreciate you sharing your story with me. But I feel like I didn't get to hear the rest of it." I said.

"Well, Shawn, it is quite a story, and it is sad to say it is all true. Every word. There is a lot of the story left to tell. The good news is that it has a happy ending." He smiled. "Why don't we set a time to call each other, and I can tell you the rest of the story."

"I'd like that, Joe." I shook his hand and held it a little longer than I maybe should have.

This is the incredibly true story of a man named Joe Townsend, a man I am proud to call friend. He is an amazing man of courage and grace. I would like to be half the man he is, and I am working on that.

I am a motivational speaker, but in this case, the tables have been turned. Joe's story of adversity and challenges has *motivated me* deeply.

I believe there are some powerful lessons for all of us to learn in Joe's story. I think that the story of *The Soul Survivor* will not only help us *survive,* but *thrive* in our own lives. It will help us soar and take off to new heights.

As Cavett Robert once said,

> If we study the lives of great men and women carefully and unemotionally we find that, invariably, greatness was developed, tested and revealed through the darker periods of their lives. One of the largest tributaries of the river of greatness is always the stream of adversity.[3]

Let's start the story in the beginning, which of course is where every story should start.

ENDNOTES

1. Michael Altshuler, quoted on *Famous Quotes & Quotations;* http://www.famous-quotes-and-quotations.com/michael_altshuler.html; accessed May 18, 2011.

2. John Gillespie Magee, Jr., "High Flight," *Arlington National Cemetery Website*; http://www.arlingtoncemetery.net/highflig.htm; accessed May 18, 2011.

3. Cavett Robert, quoted on *Thinkexist.com;* http://thinkexist.com/quotation/if_we_study_the_lives_of_great_men_and_women/296966.html; accessed May 18, 2011.

Chapter 2

Joe (Not John) 3:16

If a child is to keep his inborn sense of wonder, he needs the companionship of at least one adult who can share it, rediscovering with him the joy, excitement and mystery of the world we live in.
—Rachel Carson[1]

I thought about Joe Townsend a lot over the next two weeks. I didn't want to. I mean, I had plenty to do, but every time I found myself in a quiet moment while driving down the road, I would think about him and Kelley and his girls. In fact, I couldn't get him off my mind because his story was so amazing and heartfelt and real. It wrapped around my head and heart, and it wouldn't let go. Sometimes a story just finds you.

They say that your life can change in the blink of an eye. Everyone has faced some sort of adversity if they have lived long enough. Just like everyone else, I have certainly experienced adversity. I have faced crushing financial difficulties, been physically injured, and survived a disease that sometimes kills people. Early in my married life, my wife and I lost a child named Lauren Sue. Our daughter was stillborn due to a cord accident in the uterus. After we discovered that Lauren was no longer alive, we had to go through 23 hours of labor to deliver the baby. That was devastating. It was the most difficult experience we had ever had, and it was awful and tragic. I still remember a very kind nurse telling me quietly "God doesn't give things to people unless they can handle it."

So I guess I have my battle scars. We all do. No one has lived a life free of adversity, and if you have, you are one lucky person. As difficult as all of those experiences were, and believe me when I say they were enormously trying and difficult, they did not hold a candle to the horrific events of Joe's life. If my adversities were a candle, his were a raging, hot, orange inferno. It still amazes me when I think about the fact that the furnace of adversity didn't consume Joe entirely.

Several weeks after we met, Joe sent me pictures of the plane. In one, the plane was covered by a bright blue tarp. The next photo was shocking. The tarp was off, and the wreckage was so bad that I could not believe any human being walking on earth could have survived that kind of crash. I could see a white plane with a beautiful blue graphic stripe. That is one of the only parts that is recognizable as part of a plane. It was a tangled mess of metal, which looked less like a plane crash and more like an explosion.

The two wings were snapped and torn apart, and the entire front of the plane was a gaping hole of twisted metal. My mouth fell open in shocked amazement and horror. By looking at the wreckage, I could imagine the destruction and the fatalities, but it was incomprehensible how Joe even survived.

When Joe and I met on the flight to Florida, he was cheerful, upbeat, and obviously still an optimistic person. He had energy and smiled a lot. I found myself wondering how I would have responded in the same situation. How would I respond if I was critically injured, lost my way of making a living, and lost my entire family? I would like to say I would be strong and survive and thrive, but I don't know. It would be foolish to imagine that's how I would react. You can't really know unless you have lived it. I have heard people at funerals talking to the bereaved family and saying, "I know how you feel." No, you don't! If you are ever in that situation, you should never say, "I know how you feel," because you really don't. You have no right to say it. You couldn't possibly know how the other person feels. So the best approach is just to say, "I'm sorry. How can I help you?"

Here is what is ironic. I am a motivational speaker. I have written several books about motivation, and it is a topic that I'm most passionate about. I have done a lot of research relating to motivation and initiative. But here is the big question: Would I have the iron will, the mettle, the strength, the internal fortitude, the faith to believe that someday it would all be OK again? Would I recover and regain my sense of optimism? I just don't know. That is the truth of the matter. So when we each look at the story of Joe Townsend and the massive adversity that he faced, we can learn something about our own lives. And, perhaps most importantly, we can learn thoughts and approaches to use when we face some type of adversity.

So why is Joe such an optimist? Maybe John Burroughs said it best:

> Temperament lies behind mood; behind will, lies the fate of character. Then behind both, the influence of family the tyranny of culture; and finally the power of climate and environment; and we are free, only to the extent we rise above these.[2]

Somehow, some way, Joe was able to rise above, like a solo pilot in a bright, white glider plane soaring above the canyons in a crystal-blue sky—free and above adversity. He rose above it.

Joe and I set up a time to talk by phone, and I was really looking forward to talking to him. It was kind of like *Tuesday's with Morrie,* except it was Thursday, and I was talking to Joe, and he doesn't plan on dying anytime soon.

The phone rang. I looked at the caller ID on the phone and knew immediately who it was.

"Hello?" I said.

"Hidey Ho, Shawn! This is Joe."

"Well hello, Captain Townsend."

He chuckled and said, "Well thank you for the respect. Unfortunately, I am not actively flying as a captain anymore due to my injuries. But thanks. It sounds real nice to be called captain, and I miss flying. It was a lot of fun training to become captain." I detected a wistful tone in his voice.

I told him I was delighted to speak with him again and I wanted to hear the rest of the story. I wanted to know how he got to be the person he was, and I wanted to understand what gave him the strength to survive and thrive despite all that he had lost.

"Well, how much do you want to know, and where do ya wanna start?" Joe asked.

I smiled and said, "Start at the beginning."

"OK."

You will learn more about this, but faith and lack of faith have always been a part of my life in one way or another. My life has been complicated and messy with many twists and turns, but I will explain more about that later.

It is very ironic that my great grandfather's name was Repentance Townsend. Yep, that's right. I know it sounds like I'm making this up, because his name sounds like that of a Hollywood movie character. I'm sure he was a character, but he really was named Repentance! His parents were obviously people of faith, and he emigrated from Sheffield, England to Norfolk, Virginia in 1725. That is all we know about him. We don't even have a picture of him. I wish I did. Sometimes, when I am daydreaming and I let my mind wander, I often think of him as Daniel Day Lewis in a dusty suit, arriving at the docks in Norfolk, looking at his new home—America. He is, in some ways, the theological thread that binds my family's faith together.

I was born on a cold, dark, stormy night—just kidding! I have no idea what the weather was like, and I don't remember it. I was a little too young. It may have been raining, because it was spring—March 16, to be exact, in 1958, in the town of Winston-Salem, North Carolina. So this is where truth starts to sound like fiction. Yes, I was born on 3-16, and for those who know the Bible, John 3:16 is probably one of the most significant verses in the entire Bible. So what do you guess my parents, who are strong believers in God, would name me? John, right?

Nope. What do my parents name me? Joe! My parents name me Joe. Now, if a person had a boy on 3:16, wouldn't it make sense to name him *John?* Hello? My parents waited until they had another son, and they named *him* John and he *wasn't* born on 3:16! That always kind of stuck in my craw. But I am not bitter about it or anything. Think how easy it would have been, however, to remember my birthday—"When is John's birthday? Duh! March 16!" I never heard any stories about my birth, so it must have been uneventful. I know this one thing: I was smiling. I am always smiling, and people tell me I always have a great smile on my face. As the T-shirt line says, "life is good," and I still believe that today. That is why I smile, and I am not apologizing for it. I am a shameless optimist.

My parents are Al and Betty Townsend. If Hollywood were to cast my dad, Alan Alda, known for his role as Hawkeye Pierce on the television show *M*A*S*H,* would play him. My dad was six feet tall, had hazel eyes and a slender build, and was very fit because he loved to play tennis.

My mom was short and had short, curly, dark hair. She would be played by Doris Roberts, known for her role as Raymond's mom on the television show "*Everybody Loves Raymond.*" Like Raymond's mom, my mother was a very complex individual with many sides to her that, to this day, I still don't understand.

I was one of six children, and my mom thought having kids was her divine calling. I had four sisters and one brother. This calling took a toll on her. During the Winston-Salem years, she suffered from postpartum depression, an affliction that was not well understood at the time. She actually had a breakdown and was taken to an inpatient mental-health facility. She was having visions and hearing voices from God in her mind and in her sad state was making references to "drowning the kids because they would be better off in Heaven." It reminds me of that Andrea Yates case a few years ago, which still gives me chills when I think about it.

My mom was hospitalized for three long months, but recovered and triumphed over depression and eventually went on to have three more kids. She never had the symptoms again. Keep in mind that this was in the late '50s, an era in which people really did not understand a lot about post-partum depression and its effective treatment. No one really understood why my mom was so depressed. So I guess the gumption or perseverance I have is from my mom. My mom never gave in and my mom never gave up. Ever.

When I was in kindergarten, I was a little bit shy. For some reason, I was frightened about the idea of being around a bunch of people that I didn't know. Shortly after the school year started, I politely asked the teacher if I could be excused to go to the bathroom. She said that I could. When I got out of the classroom, I ran to my house, which was conveniently across the street from the school. Unfortunately, my plan did not work, because my mom made me go back. I tried this approach several times, but each time my mom would make me go back to class, and I figured out then and there that I couldn't get out of school no matter what I tried.

My mom always fixed us a delicious Sunday dinner, and then our big family liked to watch television together in the evening. I sat on a big, beige couch, and it had a blue and green leaf pattern on it. Back when television was a three-channel universe, I think every family in America was watching television on Sunday nights. My dad would fix popcorn, and we would all gather around our huge, wooden console television and watch *Disney's Wonderful World of Color*. I always loved how Uncle Walt introduced the program while sitting at his desk in his office. I always felt like he was talking directly to me.

Mutual of Omaha's Wild Kingdom with Marlin Perkins was always fascinating, with Marlin's stilted promotions for Mutual of Omaha: "Yes, the porcupine protects *his family* with his quills. That is why you too should protect *your* family with our life insurance." I also used to chuckle as Marlin would stand in the foreground talking about alligators, well out of harm's way, while his co-host Jim was wrestling a 12-foot-long alligator in the mud and getting his butt kicked. Marlin would smile and say, "Get them, Jim!" Of course, he never bothered to help. We also loved *The Ed Sullivan Show*, with his regular guest Topo Gigio and of course the Beatles and Elvis Presley. There was nothing better than the great western *Bonanza* with Ben Cartwright and sons Adam, Little Joe, and Hoss. Those were the days when things were more simple and maybe more pure. Maybe they just seemed that way.

My dad worked as an engineer at Western Electric in Winston-Salem, at Pan American Services at Patrick Air Force Base, and he retired from RCA (later to become General Electric). My mom, typical for that time, stayed home with the kids. I thought my dad had the coolest job in the world as an engineer at a big company. He had a very strong work ethic and hardly ever missed a day of work, as he wanted to provide for his family. Because my dad was an engineer, I remember that he always dressed business casual. Well, they didn't call it that back then, but you know what I mean. He usually wore solid color shirts and slacks, but he always looked sharp because of his slim build. I always knew when my dad had an important meeting at work because he wore a tie on those days. I looked up to him, and in fact, I wanted to be him. He was my hero.

My dad was the strong, silent type who never said very much. He was rugged like Gary Cooper or John Wayne. Maybe he would have been a good western movie star. He never really told me why he was quiet, but I know it was because of the way that he was raised. Dad grew up in Arkansas and had a very difficult life and childhood. Sadly, his mom was a diabetic, and she died when he was only ten years old. Fortunately, his beloved Aunt Halley took him in and raised him as her own from that point on. She was the sweetest lady to ever come out of the state of Mississippi, and my dad always felt very blessed to have her in his life.

In many ways, the things that he taught me were not through his words, but through his actions. To loosely paraphrase Stephen Covey, "It's not what you say that people learn from, it's what you do."[3] Of course, back then no one had ever heard of Stephen Covey, and he hadn't written *The 7 Habits of Highly Effective People* yet, but my dad was already living the principles. His personal principle was that talk was cheap. We connected not by talking, but by doing things together.

I'm struck by how much time I wanted to spend with my dad as a child, and I guess that is the ultimate compliment. At a certain point, I got good enough to be his tennis partner, and we used to play doubles with his friends. He put up a basketball hoop in the backyard patio, and my siblings and our friends would play classic games like horse with him. My dad liked to work on cars and taught me how to work on them as well. We would work on cars for hours at a time. It was a guy thing to do, and it was really the perfect father-and-son activity. We worked on old Jaguars, my Datsun 2000, and believe it or not, an old 1945 Willys Sedan Delivery Wagon that I bought. When needed, we even worked on two Volkswagen Beetle convertibles that belonged to my sisters Rosie and Margie. The floorboards were made of a thin metal, and my experience with repairing my fiberglass surfboards came in handy in rebuilding their floor pans.

Because my dad was a kind and compassionate man, I was determined to be just like him. You could say that I got a lot of qualities from my dad, namely the quality of being outgoing and friendly. I have never met a stranger. It would not be within the core of my personality to get on a plane and not speak with the passengers to my left and my right. It would just seem rude somehow. So that is the kind of influence that my dad had on me.

My mom was a study in complexity. She was a real puzzle. For every side A of her, there was a side B, for every *ying* there was a *yang*, and for every rule there was an exception. Just when you thought you had her figured out, she would do the opposite of what you expected. My mom was a stay-at-home mom during all the years of my childhood, but she hardly ever stayed at home. She wasn't out drinking or gallivanting. She was out fulfilling her mission and *saving the downtrodden of the world.*

She probably could have had a uniform and a cape, because she was Superwoman, at least in my mind. My mom was the most determined person I have ever known, and her purpose or mission in life was to save others. She was determined and focused and would never take no for an answer. My mom was God's steamroller (now there is an idea for a super-hero). If somebody got in her way, she would roll right over them, including members of her family. She was a very religious woman, a Catholic, and went to mass two or three times every day throughout my childhood.

She had many different colored rosary beads, and some of them were really cool wooden ones. I remember distinctly that every time we would go on a trip in the car, she pulled out her rosary beads and would say the rosary and insisted that we say a rosary too. Her deep fervor for the Catholic Church never diminished over the entire course of her life. I know that my mom's religious devotion may seem to be a great thing, but like I said, for every good attribute in her there was a bad one. Ironically, the good in her was often also the bad. Her unending devotion to the Church and to her causes really had a negative impact on me.

See, my mom didn't belong to me or to my sisters and brother. When we had her, she was just on loan to us; we knew that pretty soon she would be back to the church again. She had to share herself with the rest of the world. It was not an option; it was an obsession. It's hard for me to say, but at various times in my childhood life, I felt neglected. Why? I felt like every church event and activity took precedence over me. Don't get me wrong. I am very proud of her accomplishments, but there were times when I wished that she just stayed home more. I needed a mom. As a result of the time my mom spent on her religious causes, I always felt like she was in her own little world, and I never felt close to her, or maybe she never let me be close to her. I was an observer not a participant. Sadly, there was never really any point in my life when this feeling changed.

We moved to Melbourne, Florida, when I was almost four years old. Our house there had a huge backyard, and that is where I took my first step toward manhood. I learned how to ride a bike when I was five years old. As I rode my orange Stingray bike, my dad would run beside me and hold onto the handlebars to keep me from falling over. As I picked up speed, he would let go, sometimes without me knowing it, and off I would go. Learning to ride a bike gave me a newfound freedom, and a whole new world opened up to me. I could ride all over the neighborhood and beyond. I know that sounds incredibly dangerous today, but that's what kids did back then. We rode anywhere and everywhere on our bikes. In later years, my bike became a delivery vehicle for my paper route. To me, my bike was about speed and freedom. When I think about it, some of the key themes of my life are speed and freedom. I guess I'm the kind of guy who likes to feel the wind running through my hair. That's probably why I have always been attracted to cars and planes.

When I was around eight years old, my dad took me out fishing with his friend Bob Schneider. Bob was one of my favorites. He was a happy go lucky guy, muscular in shape, and about 6 feet tall with dark hair. He was the kind of adult who would actually speak to children, and he had a good sense of humor. That day, we went outside of the Sebastian Inlet in a boat, and we had an amazing day of fishing. We were catching one bluefish after another. It was the kind of day when you almost wonder if the fish would bite an empty hook.

I will never forget that particular day. The waves on the ocean were little bit rough. They were about 5 to 7 feet high. If you have ever piloted a boat, you know that one of the key rules when you are drifting is to keep your bow pointed into the wave. But that day, our boat turned sideways because my dad and Bob were too excited pulling in their haul. As fate would have it, a large wave flipped the boat over, and we were all thrown into deep water as the boat capsized. I don't know if you've ever been suddenly dumped into the water, but it is always a shock. To this day, I still remember being deep underwater and not knowing which way was up or down or sideways. As I was panicking and looking around in the water, I looked up and suddenly saw the greatest sight I had ever seen—my dad. He dove down to rescue me, and to me, he looked like the proverbial Superman coming down to swoop me up to safety. I never would have made it without him. My dad took me to the shore, which was an easy swim because he was in great physical condition and the tide was coming in.

When we arrived at the shore looking like soaked rats, there were several people on shore watching. I will never forget a nice woman who took me to her truck camper. She was slender, about 5 feet 5 inches tall, and had sun-bleached hair—the kind you see on people who have spent a lot of time outdoors. Even though I did not know her and she was a stranger to me, she took me to her truck camper. She had a son about my age who was out fishing with his dad, and she gave me some of his dry clothes to put on. She asked me if I was hungry, and I nodded my head as I shivered. She cooked me a hot dog. To this day, I'm not sure what brand of hot dog it was or how she fixed it. But I'll say this: it was the best hot dog, bite for bite, that I have ever tasted or ever will. It's funny how food always seems to taste better shortly after defying death.

My dad went to help Bob with the boat and returned later to pick me up, thanking the woman for the clothing and for feeding me while he was gone. So the lesson that I learned from my dad is that dads will risk their own lives to save their children. Every now and then, I pick up the paper or see a story on network news about people abusing children. I just can't understand it. How can someone be mean to a child? In my opinion, someone being mean to a child must have a heart of stone, and it is something I just can't imagine.

In my mother's mission to save and minister to those in need, she often would allow strangers to stay with us at our house. Yes, that's right—strangers! Can you imagine coming home as a kid from school and realizing that there is a total stranger living in your house that your mom picked up off the street? This was not uncommon in our home. As a kid, I was completely puzzled by this approach. Where in the world did these people come from? Why were they living in our house? It was generally because my mom had met them somewhere and felt she could help them.

At one point, an older lady, Loretta, needed a place to live, so my mom took her in as our cook. Just took her in. Loretta was the typical grandma type, around 75 years old, about 4 feet 10 inches tall, and of course had graying hair. As it turns out, she had a very interesting background. She used to be a cook for the Henry Ford family on the island of Palm Beach. She stayed with us for about a year before moving back to Detroit where she had friends who were working for the Ford family there. We loved having her living with us for one selfish reason: we loved her cooking. The woman could flat-out cook. Her cooking was a true blessing, because my mom could burn a piece of meat better than anybody. Maybe that's why I still love my steak well-done!

When I was about 14, my mom met Kevin, a homeless drug addict. He was a drifter who looked like he had lived a rough life. He was 5 feet 9 inches tall, had sandy hair, and was tan and had a muscular build. He was just the type that my mom felt that she could save. Did she ever think about the danger of this approach? Maybe. In my opinion, she probably thought about the danger, but concluded that the mission was more important than the potential danger that it created for her family. She just had a heart of gold when it came to helping others. Mom met him through a friend across the street. My mom, with her religious fervor, was determined to rehabilitate him, to save him, and to get him to church, but he was a con artist of the highest order. He would tell her everything she wanted to hear and would con my parents out of money, including a frequent $20 for a fix.

Now, they didn't know what a fix was, but everybody else knew what the money was for. I guess my mom's religious fervor blinded her to other people's ill intentions. I vividly remember being alone with Kevin when he was rolling up his sleeve, tying a tube around his tan arm, and injecting heroin into one of his ropy veins. He did this right in front of me. Unbelievable! We had a heroin addict living in our house! He even stole my shiny green Schwinn Varsity 10-speed bike that I purchased with my hard earned dishwasher pay from Howley's Restaurant and sold it for a few hits of heroin. It made me furious that he was taking advantage of my family and me. What was I going to do? I was a kid. No one listens to a kid. He rotated in and out of our lives for many years.

My mom missed out on spending quality time with us after school because she spent an hour each day at the church, which was across the street from our house. From 3:00 to 4:00 o'clock she observed a "holy hour," where she was involved in prayer and could not be disturbed. So when I got home from school, I did not have a mom who encouraged me to hit the books and study after school. It was really left up to our own initiative (or lack of initiative). She usually arrived home around 4:30 in the afternoon and started preparing dinner so it would be on the table when my Dad came home. It was kind of like a dysfunctional *Leave It to Beaver* show.

Even though the kids in the family did not get a lot of her attention, she accomplished a lot of amazing things in the communities where we lived. She shared her faith with everyone, whether they were migrant farm workers, homeless drug addicts, or wayward lost souls. One great accomplishment was that she set up a free day-care center for migrant farm workers so that their children would have a place to come to during the day while their parents labored in the fields. Mom also started a jail ministry for teenage girls in a juvenile detention center and led a Bible study in there. A talented keyboardist, she played the organ Monday through Friday for the residents of a local Catholic nursing home. It is amazing one person can do so much. She was a whirling dervish with Catholic fervor.

My mom was a world champion to the outside world, but that consumed a lot of her time. When I was a boy, I thought it was pretty cool to be able to run my own life without a lot of interference. I loved having that kind of freedom, but that came at a cost because, like most kids, I made lots of stupid mistakes and my parents were generally too busy to notice or guide me through them. In hindsight, I always felt that my mother had too much going on in her life and that I was not first, second, or third priority to her. I know that is probably not a fair statement, but I really felt that I was not a priority at all. I was not able to verbalize it as a child, but I realize now that I felt a tremendous amount of distance from my mother. Those feelings would have a huge impact on my adult life when it came time for me to pick a wife.

Later on in life, I would question why a church would encourage a mother with six children at home to devote so very much of her time to religious endeavors. I often wondered why at some point the priest or a nun didn't take her aside and say, "You're going to mass too much. You need to stay home with your children." Maybe they thought she could be a supermom and do it all. Maybe they thought the church was more important. I don't really know why.

There were a few times that I remember my mom making a sacrifice for me, like when it rained and I had to deliver papers for my paper route. My mom would always drive me in the car on the weekdays if it was raining. If it was raining on a weekend, my dad would drive. That was nice. Today, I think about my love affair with cars and wonder if it's connected to the good feelings that I retained from my mom driving me around in those early days.

I think my mom had a need to be involved in the church, and this need was like a powerful magnet. The need was so strong that she was unable or unwilling to control it or moderate it. Some people might call it selfishness, although that might raise a few eyebrows, because she was involved in doing God's work and not her own. It really is a hard issue to define. Where does one draw the line between devotion and selfishness? Sometimes, when I'm sitting in front of the fire in my living room in Colorado at night, I think about this and am never able to narrow it down. But I do know one thing, that as a child I felt in my heart that my mother was more devoted to her causes than she was to our family. Little Joey needed a Mom who was around more than she was.

I do have fond memories of our childhood and of spending time together as a family. We had a big family including Mom, Dad, Mary Anne, Albert Joseph, Elizabeth Marie, Rose Marie, John Charles, and Margaret Mary. There was no John boy, but it does kind of sound like a Catholic version of *The Waltons*. With six kids in private school for 12 years, I can't imagine my parents having much extra money left, but we did take vacations. They were always fun times. We would take vacations in the summers to the Blue Ridge Mountains of North Carolina, as well as other trips to see relatives in Mississippi, Arkansas, and Texas.

I have very fond memories of stopping for picnics along the way and reaching into a silver metal cooler filled with food and drinks. This was of course to save money (feeding a family of eight was very expensive in a restaurant), but it was a lot more fun than eating at a restaurant. These picnics were some of the very best times for me, because my mom would be totally disengaged from her ministry work. All of us kids had her complete and undivided attention. At those times, my mom could be very loving because she didn't have any distractions around her. I remember her being very happy during these picnics. Enjoying a picnic with my mom was the best way to be in her life. Even today, you don't have to ask me twice to have a picnic. I love picnics!

My mom was very ingenious at saving money, and she always brought along an electric fry pan with us so that she could fix bacon and eggs in the morning in the hotel room. I still love the smell of frying bacon.

My dad did most of the driving and used to get tired so we would stop driving around 6 PM. In my later teen years, my mom would occasionally help with the driving, probably so that she could get a break from trying to contain six kids. She had a lead foot, and like in the movie *Top Gun*, she was feeling the need for speed. The apple did not fall far from that tree, for I love speed.

We would always find a motel with a pool! We didn't have a pool at home, and while on vacation, we always loved swimming in a pool. After a tough day traveling on the road, there was never a more exciting sight then seeing the dark aqua blue of the pool. We would have great fun swimming and playing games that required no equipment, like Marco Polo. We would stay in the pool until our fingers looked like wrinkled prunes. Then, of course, we would sit around endlessly fascinated by our "prune fingers." Every time I smell chlorine, or the sweet scent of wet towels, I think about those days.

My dad was a gentle man, but he also stood for principles. He rarely raised his voice. I do remember that he did one time when our family was having a picnic lunch at Lantana Beach. Some young, smart-aleck teenage boys who sat near us were snickering and making loud derogatory comments about girls as they walked by. Finally, my dad had enough, stood up, and went over to the boys. He told them in a tough tone that they had better stop talking that way, because it was disrespectful and there were young children there. His tough tone and angry facial expression were all it took for them to stop. I learned an important lesson while observing my dad stand up for what was right. I know that in this world there are issues that are gray or ambiguous, but there are some things that just aren't right, and I'm willing to take a stand when people are doing wrong.

Sometimes when I think about my childhood, I remember bits and pieces of great memories almost as if I'm looking through a file cabinet of 8mm films. I remember my dad taking me out sailing with one of his workmates in the Intracoastal Waterway, when we found a sandbar and the skeg stopped us abruptly. When the tide came, and we were freed loose, we made it to the Palm Beach Inlet into the Atlantic Ocean. It was a beautiful day—the waves were around 2 feet high, the sky was Hope-Diamond blue, and the sun sent a little white sparkle off of everything it touched. As we sailed swiftly with the boat leaning with a light breeze, the sails flapped open like fresh laundry on the line, and smiling porpoises came along the side of the boat to check us out and race along with us. It was the perfect Hollywood scene with the exquisite casting of Mother Nature.

When I was a kid, I was always looking for different ways to make money. In 1967 my dad took a new job in West Palm Beach where I began fourth grade. When I was old enough to mow the lawn, I earned my first income. I mowed not only our lawn, but other lawns in the neighborhood as well. I was quite the little entrepreneur. At 11 years old, I took the ultimate entrepreneurial adventure for a kid: a paper route. As a little 11-year-old boy trying to ride a bike with a basket full of heavy newspapers, I learned quickly about the science of balance. My cool new favorite bike (my huffy Orange Crush with the banana seat and the ape hanger handlebars) was a little top heavy. I, unfortunately, learned this lesson the hard way.

When I was still a rookie paperboy, I took a curve too sharply a couple of times and the weight of the papers tipped my orange stingray bike right onto its side very quickly. I would fall over, and papers would scatter all over the street. This was really irritating because I was damaging my inventory, which could cut into my profits. I was always very determined, though. Instead of running home crying, I would wipe away my tears, lick the wounds on my knuckles, and dust off my knees. Then I would slowly gather up every single paper. I would gently dust them off, reassemble them, carefully put them back into the basket on my bike, and go back to work. For some reason, I knew that I couldn't stop; I couldn't give up. My nature has always been to never give up, and that nature is what I had in me when I was in a wheelchair. With my wife and sweet angels gone, it would have been very easy and understandable to give up.

I never, never, never give up. I hadn't really learned much about Winston Churchill as a young boy, so I guess I didn't learn it from him. But it isn't surprising that the son of Betty Townsend would be determined to persevere. On rainy days, when mom or dad would drive me on my route, I would stand on the station wagon tailgate pitching papers, and I learned an important lesson about accuracy. I learned that the closer the paper was to the door, the better the tips I would get from my customers. A happy customer was a generous customer.

All of my school years, from kindergarten through high school, were spent in Catholic institutions. My mom was determined that all of her children receive a private Catholic education regardless of the cost. One day, at Saint Juliana's Catholic middle school, I was sitting in the back of the classroom with some of my buddies, Dan, Mike, Joe, and Benny. We were smart alecks and were being disruptive in the class. We knew we were in trouble when we got *that look* from the teacher. The teacher marched us down the long corridor to the stairwell and down the next corridor to the principal's office. If you saw us from a distance, you would think you were watching condemned men walking to the gas chamber. We knew what was coming. We were getting ready to experience a significant attitude adjustment.

We sat down in Sister Anne Damien's office, and our teacher described what we had done. We all sat with our heads bowed reverently, hoping that our remorseful facial expressions and body language would allow us to escape our punishment. But that was not to be. Sister Damien proceeded to lecture and berate us about our appalling misbehavior. Then came the most important part—corporal punishment to teach us a lesson. Boy, did she teach a lesson. Sister Anne Damien had in her possession a very special punishment device: a wooden paddle. This was not just any wooden paddle; this was a paddle specially modified for the job with holes drilled into it to lessen the wind resistance.

Each of us had to individually bend over a chair, hold onto the arms of that chair, while our backsides were pummeled with the huge paddle.

Let's put it this way; if Sister Damien were a baseball player, she would have been in the Hall of Fame for the force and energy of her swing. With each swing, she would knock the ball out of the park. If she had been a golfer, she would have won the world driving championship for distance. Each stroke of the paddle made a loud whooping sound when it landed, and softly whooshed as Sister Damien pulled it back up to deliver another blow. It brought tears not only my eyes, but to the eyes of all of the bad boys.

I know that corporal punishment has fallen into disfavor today. Many parents and authority figures do not believe in spanking. I can only tell you that I was blessed that day. Don't get me wrong; I don't like pain. But that day, I learned a lesson about being disruptive and disrespectful, and it was the lesson that I needed as a young boy. To this day, when I'm at a social function and someone is being loud or disruptive, I give him or her the "hairy eyeball." This is a look designed to put someone in his or her place without saying a word.

As far as my involvement with religion as a child, I would say it was really more about obligation and trying to keep my mom happy than about inspiration. I was the proverbial altar boy and had to learn prayers at the foot of the altar and Latin from the head priest, Monsignor McGrenahan. I didn't really get much out of it. I was more or less going through the motions. I think that my mom's fervent commitment to Catholicism created in me a resistance to religion or at least to the Catholic religion. It would not be until much later on in my life that religion began to have a much deeper meaning. To me, attending church as a child was just an endless series of sit-stand-kneel, and it had little personal significance for me.

So what did I learn from my childhood? In school we used to build rings out of brightly colored strips of construction paper. We would then take these loops and connect them to make long colorful chains that stretched across the room. My childhood was like that. Each loop was a distinct moment. Each loop was an experience and lesson that helped create the person that I am today.

I am fully convinced in my heart, and in my soul, that every one of these experiences caused me to be successful as I traveled the road of life and made me able to survive and thrive during my darkest times.

I am thankful for my mom and dad who taught me many great lessons and for the nuns and priests who steered the young Joe in the right direction, even when I was unable to appreciate the lesson at the time. I am grateful for the friends and family who contributed to the fabric of who I am. I love them all.

I am Joe Townsend, and my experiences have made me who I am today.

I had listened very carefully to Joe's stories about his childhood. I was wildly curious to see what had happened in his childhood that prepared him to be *The Soul Survivor.* To me it was like staring into a string of Joe's DNA under an electron microscope to figure out how those chains were assembled. Sure there was the genetic part handed down by the gene pool. But what about his experience DNA? What were the events that shaped him? What did he learn that developed within his very core this remarkable iron will? Some people have it—but where does it come from? Why do other people who seem really strong collapse under adversity? I don't know. For Joe, it seems that all of his experiences and all of his teachers and people he knew taught him different lessons. He was able to take all those lessons and weave them into a core belief—a philosophy of persistence that made him strong enough to be who he is and to survive and thrive. I felt so honored at that point, realizing I had the awesome task of helping him tell the story. "Wow! Joe, that was great hearing all about your childhood," I said when he had finished.

"Thanks, Shawn. I hope I didn't bore you to death," he replied.

"No, Joe, not at all," I said. "In fact, I find all of this very fascinating, because it really gives me insight into who you are and how you were able to survive the losses that you went through."

"Which brings me to my next point," said Joe.

"Which is?"

"I've talked to you three times now, and I have decided I want you to help me write a book about adversity."

"Excuse me?" I replied. I was a little bit shocked.

"Yep, I think you're the perfect person to help me write my book. I have always wanted to tell my story to help inspire others. I know it sounds a little corny, but I think that's part of the reason I survived."

"Boy, Joe, that is a big honor, and I am so pleased that you feel like I am the one to tell your story. I must tell you though that I have a really busy business as a speaker and trainer, and I'm not sure if I have the time."

"That's all right. I understand," said Joe. "Just give it some thought and let me know. Then we can take it from there."

"Okay, I'll give it some thought," I said.

"But, Joe, when will I hear the rest of your story?"

"I would be happy to share it with you whenever you like."

"Let's figure out a time when we can talk next week."

"Okey dokey, Smokey."

"I have to give you credit, Captain Joe. You have a wicked sense of humor."

"As a told you, I was born smiling, and I have been smiling ever since."

"See ya, Joe."

"Adios, Amigo Shawn."

ENDNOTES

1. Rachel Carson, *The Sense of Wonder* (New York: HarperCollins, 1965).

2. John Burroughs, 1837–1921, American naturalist and author, quoted in *Book of Famous Quotes;* http://www.famous-quotes.com/author.php?aid=1174; accessed May 18, 2011.

3. Steven Covey, *The 7 Habits of Highly Effective People: Powerful Lessons in Personal Change* (New York: Free Press, 1990).

Chapter 3

Beaches, Bikes, and Acrobats

The sculptor will chip off all unnecessary material to set free the angel. Nature will chip and pound us remorselessly to bring out our possibilities. She will strip us of wealth, humble our pride, humiliate our ambition, let us down from the ladder of fame, will discipline us in a thousand ways, if she can develop a little character, Everything must give way to that. Wealth is nothing, position is nothing, fame is nothing, manhood is everything.—Orison Swett Marden[1]

The phone rang in my office.

"Hello?"

"Hidey Ho, Mr. Shawn!" I recognized the voice immediately. It was Joe.

"Hey, Joe. How are you doing?"

"I am doing fabulous!" He said with his usual enthusiasm.

"So, what's going on?" I said.

"Oh, I had a great weekend. I flew down to Florida for a few days to visit with my dad and to have lunch with a few friends."

"Joe, it seems like every time I talk to you, you're having lunch with a friend."

"That is probably true," he said chuckling. "You know, Shawn, all my life I've been blessed to have very good friends. I have hundreds of good friends and many more casual friends. You, Shawn, are my new good friend," Joe said graciously.

"That's great, Joe. Although I can't say that I'm surprised," I replied.

"So, Shawn, did you decide? You know, about helping me write about my adversity?" Joe asked.

"Yep, I sure did. Here is what I would like to do, Joe. I understand how books are sold, and how the publishing world works. I'm going to write a sample chapter with your input, and I will draft a book proposal that we can use to sell the book."

So why did I agree to write the book? I was very busy. I had a thriving speaking and training business, and I had ten books of my own. When we first met on the plane, I was upgraded, and Joe was given a ticket by US Air with an upgrade. In a nutshell, neither one of us were supposed to be there. I should have been back in coach and Joe somewhere back in coach. Of all the seats on that plane, somehow fate or chance or destiny (or God's will?) had thrown us together in that plane. I don't really know why. When I heard Joe's story, I was deeply touched. I felt compelled to help him tell it—and to share the powerful message with the world. Besides, Joe has such a good heart and he is so real, I just can't tell him no. I was hooked.

"That is great news, Shawn! When can we get started?" Joe replied enthusiastically.

"The sooner the better. Now that I am writing your book, I will have to pay careful attention when you talk," I said laughing. "Do you have a title in mind?" I asked.

He responded back immediately: "The Soul SURVIVOR!"

"Wow. I like that title. It has a double meaning. How did you come up with it?"

"Well, there is kind of a cool little history lesson behind it. Dating way before recorded time, the maritime industry started counting the souls on board a ship before they left their port. They still do this today. Back in the early days of sailing, conditions on board a ship were not very sanitary. Many of the crew and passengers would acquire fatal diseases like dysentery and malaria. Medical care was primitive in those days, and they would throw the dead overboard. They did this to prevent the further spread of disease on their long voyages at sea, which could be several months or more. When they arrived at their destination, the crew would count the living souls on board.

"This practice has crossed over into air travel. On every flight, whether it be a small aircraft with one soul on board or an airliner with many, the number of people aboard is given to the Federal Aviation Administration (FAA), so that they have a record of how many souls were on that flight in the event of a mishap where some do not survive. One of the required fields on a flight plan asks you to list the number aboard. In the event of an emergency in flight, the Air Traffic Control (ATC) will ask these following questions, 'Aircraft (name), state the nature of your emergency and souls on board.'"

"So, Joe, a government form has a line on it that says 'Souls on Board'?" I asked curiously.

"No, the form asks for the number aboard. It is only when you declare an emergency with ATC that they will ask how many souls are on board."

"Oh. OK. Now we have a title, and we are ready," I replied.

"You might even have to start taking notes," he joked back in reply.

"So Joe, now that we have that straight, the last time we talked, you finished up your childhood years. But I'm really curious to know about what happened to you as a teen."

"So do you have some time now?" Joe asked.

"As a matter fact, I do. I have a feeling we're going to be spending a lot more time together!" I said.

"Yes, that certainly is true," said Joe. "Where do I start?"

I thought to myself and then said, "I already know about your childhood years, Joe. Why don't you tell me about your teen years?"

I didn't run away as a teenager, but I was always running. I was always out and about doing one of two things: playing or working. As I said in an earlier conversation, my mom and dad paid for all six of us children to be privately educated, so the only way I could have pocket money, or much else for that matter, was to earn it. The first theme that characterized my teen years was realizing that money was tight and that I would have to work for anything I wanted to do or have. But I am really glad about that, because I developed a strong work ethic at a young age. While other kids were hardly working, I was working hard. The advantage of having a great work ethic was that it helped me to become successful, and it helped me through the rehabilitation process after the crash.

When I was 13, my parents were busy feeding, clothing, and educating six kids so that, believe it or not, we didn't even have a Christmas tree. Can you imagine a family with no Christmas tree? I mean, what is Christmas without a Christmas tree? It was Christmas Eve. I had money that I had been saving from my paper route, so I took the situation into my own hands. As the old saying goes, "If it is going to be it is up to me."[2] I jumped on my bike and rode down the street about five blocks to the Christmas tree lot. With my meager paper route money, I bought a 4-foot fir tree that looked pretty pathetic, because it was one of the last trees on the lot. You could say it was almost on clearance. I was somehow able to carry it home on my bike with the end of the tree jammed into my newspaper basket. It might have been nicer than Charlie Brown's twig of a Christmas tree, but not by too much.

My sisters and I set it up in a stand and added a few Christmas decorations. To us, it was one of the most beautiful trees we had ever seen. I stood back with tears in my eyes, filled with the joy of Christmas. If that was a Hollywood movie, we would have joined hands and softly sang a Christmas carol, but it was real life, and we just stood in reverent silence enjoying the moment. There were not very many gifts to put under the tree that year, but we had the love of our family as a gift. I have always appreciated Christmas more ever since.

Many years ago, there was a movie released called *The Year of Living Dangerously*. I guess when I describe my teen years, I could say that, just like all teens who feel immortal, I had many dangerous adventures. Looking back on it now, I realize that I didn't think they were dangerous. Nope! I was just filled with the immortality and vigor of youth. It is amazing that I survived all of my adventures.

As you know, I had a paper route, and I delivered the *Palm Beach Post*. (In a weird twist of irony, years later the very same *Palm Beach Post* would publish an article about my plane crash and the funeral of my angels.) My paper route was in a modest, but nice, neighborhood behind Burger King on US Highway 1. I liked the responsibility of the paper route, and I also liked the money that it brought. It really gave me a sense of independence.

Occasionally on Saturdays, my buddy (who we knew as Danny Boy Lewis) would go with me on my route. We were about 13 years old. We weren't really kids anymore, we were really finally teenagers with changing voices and fuzzy I'm-not-sure-if-it's-there-yet mustaches. One Saturday, when we were finished delivering papers, we met up with our friend Timmy and rode over to his home. Now Danny Boy did not know where Timmy lived, and Timmy was leading the way for all of us on our bikes. When Timmy turned left into his driveway, Danny didn't realize he was turning, and Timmy slammed into Danny's front wheel. In a slow-motion circus act, Danny went flip-flopping straight into the air, flying over the handlebars at high speed and unfortunately scraped along the asphalt until he landed on his head.

Timmy and I were both stunned. We jumped off our bikes and ran over to see if Danny was OK. It was one of the strangest sights I have ever seen. Danny was unconscious, lying in the middle of the street on his back, flopping around like a fish out of water on a riverbank. It was a terrifying sight. Timmy ran into the house to call an ambulance. It was a very scary moment and one in which I felt very helpless. I had tears in my eyes as I sat watching my friend flopping around, not knowing how to help him, or if he was going to be OK.

I rode in the ambulance with Danny to Good Samaritan Hospital where, just like good Samaritans, they took him into the emergency room right away. I guess arriving in an ambulance after landing on your head gets you a do-not-pass-go, instant admittance straight into a treatment room! I waited for a couple of hours, and Danny's dad, Mr. Lewis, came to sit with me and told me how thankful he was that I was there for Danny. That felt pretty good, but I didn't do it for an accolade. I did it because Danny was my good friend. As it turned out, Danny was OK, other than a concussion and being a little warped since then. I'm kidding! (Sort of.) He's now a successful realtor with four children and a lovely bride named Liz. Danny has remained a lifelong friend, and his friendship proved vital in the days after my accident.

I always loved the beach. I love beach cars, beach music, and beach clothes. Nothing is better than the sun and the smell of Coppertone® on the beach. At the age of 14, I bought my first used surfboard, which I found in the classified advertisements of the *Palm Beach Post* for around

$20. For the younger folks reading this, we did not have Craigslist back then. We had something called classified ads that were listed in the newspaper. The newspaper was kind of like a website with news, except it was printed on paper…oh, never mind! I called it a surfboard, but really it was a longboard and looked more like a small boat. And when I say long, I'm talking 9 feet 11 inches! I guess that's why they called it a longboard. It was so long that I needed help to carry it until I got to the sand where I could drag it by one end. My parents enjoyed the beach, and my dad would dutifully pull it out of the back of the station wagon for me and help me drag it to the edge of the surf.

My next surfboard was a Roach surfboard, and it was only 6 feet 8 inches long. Let me tell you, it was a lot easier to maneuver! My surfing improved to the point where I could easily hang five, but only every now and then could I actually hang ten. Hanging ten is quite a trick. Here is how hanging ten works: you catch a good wave, and while riding the wave, you walk to the tip of the board and hang all ten toes over the edge of the board. The trick is you have to be quick about it. If you stand on the front of the board for too long, the back of the board will pop straight up in the air, and you will not so gracefully flip-flop right into the water. Hanging ten is a real accomplishment for any surfer, because you have to have the skill to make the trip to the tip and back again before the board flips. Hanging ten is a surfing badge of honor. Now you know why the Hang Ten clothing line was so popular.

As I got more into surfing, I became very adept at the things that surfers do. I became an expert at fiberglass repair and at waxing the board down with paraffin wax so that my bare feet would not slip on the wet fiberglass surface. Besides, there's not a cooler sight than a surfer waxing his board. Chicks dig it, or at least young teenage surfers think that chicks dig it. That surfboard was a chick magnet! Well, maybe not, but I like to think that it was.

I loved to surf, and I probably would have surfed more, but I did not have the luxury of being a surfing bum. After all, I didn't come from a rich family, and I had to work to make money to pay for the things that all teenagers want. I mean somebody had to pay for the bell-bottoms and the boot-cut blue jeans.

As I sat listening to Joe's teen years stories, I was really struck by his sense of adventure. He was always doing and trying something new. There was another key lesson buried in the lighthearted stories. It was the quality of persistence, the attitude of, "If this way doesn't work—I will find another way to do it, one way or another." It didn't matter what it was (a Christmas tree or surfboard), he just found a way to make it happen. This would of course pay off for him in the rest of his life. Joe was a magnet people were attracted to.

When I was about 14, we took a family vacation to South Carolina, and we stopped at a fireworks store. A teenager in a fireworks store is like a fox in the hen house or a guitarist in a music store. I loved fireworks, and my father let me bring a few back home to West Palm Beach. When we arrived, I rode my bike over to my buddy Danny's house and we were, of course, lighting off the firecrackers that I bought. It's funny that when you're a teenager, it never seems to matter that firecrackers are illegal. Most adults tend to look the other way.

After we let off a pack of about 30 firecrackers, most of the firecrackers exploded, but there were a few duds. So I sorted through them, picked up the duds, and put them into the front pocket of my T-shirt. This would turn out not to be such a good move. I soon discovered, much to my amazement, that one of them was not a dud. It just had a very stubborn, short, slow fuse. When the slow fuse reached the powder, it blew a hole right in my pocket and burned the heck out of my left chest. Since all teenagers love slapstick, none of my friends could stop laughing. Let me tell you, I had a serious case of heartburn!

I marvel at the things that I survived when I was a teenager. I would often go on boat rides with my friends Danny and Joey in Joey's 15-foot Tuppen's Torino open-bow boat. We would ride down the Intracoastal Waterway at the top speed of 30 miles an hour, and we would all jump out of the boat. At full speed.

When highway I-95 was under new construction, and before it was paved, several of us would ride on top of Danny's parents' station wagon. We blasted down the road holding on to the luggage rack for dear life. If any of our parents had seen this scene, they probably would have all had a heart attack and would have grounded us for months. But what they didn't know didn't hurt them, and fortunately for us, what we did know, we survived. My friend Danny survived those years as well as a stint in the Army and is now a university professor living in Colorado.

One weekend night, about 40 friends and I snuck into an old hotel in Palm Beach called the Biltmore. It had gone into bankruptcy many years earlier, and it was broken down, vacant, and spooky. We snuck through an open window. We walked up to the towers and down hallways. It's a wonder someone didn't fall down an elevator shaft or through rotting floorboards and kill him or herself. We even found the ballroom, and we all laughed it up and had a fun time until the cops arrived. They didn't arrest us, but they did take all of our names and reported them to the school. The next day, the Dean called us to his office for a lecture on the dangers of trespassing. We didn't think of it as trespassing; we were just having fun. The key words being *we didn't think.*

So while I was young and magnificently immortal, there were times when events sadly reminded me that life could be short. My good friend, John Hurley, was kicked out of school in the eleventh grade because he and a friend lit some powerful smoke bombs in the building on the last day of school before summer break. It was a typical teenage prank that the administration did not take lightly. (After all, they thought the building was on fire.) John was a track star, and he won many awards for long-distance running. During my senior year, John Hurley shockingly died of an aneurysm. In his brain, a tiny little artery had a bulging weak spot, and that little spot ruptured, releasing blood into his skull, silently killing him. Just like that, in the time it takes to snap your fingers, he was gone. This was incredibly shocking to me and to everyone in the school.

John Hurley was a specimen of great health and fitness. He was a nice guy, a good person. The brutal fact was that there was an earthly end that could come at any time, and it did not have to be in an airplane or an automobile. There were no warning signs that this was going to happen. No one really knows when time is going to be up. I realized, even at that young age, that life was sometimes unfair and could randomly and indiscriminately be cut short for one reason or another. Wow. That was a sobering thought. Did it make me any less reckless? No. Did it make me any less adventurous? No. It definitely did not. In fact, the feelings that I had about John made me want to seize life more, to *carpe diem*, which is Latin for *seize the day*. If life is short and brief, than I wanted to grab it and squeeze every minute out of it while I could.

In my young high school days, my buddies and I wanted to go see *Dirty Harry* starring Clint Eastwood. Of course, it was rated R, and we were under the legal age limit, so we found a way to sneak in. It's always good to have one friend that looks older, and we had one. Our good buddy Benny looked older so he bought the tickets at the box office, and we got in. I'll never forget one of Clint Eastwood's famous lines, "...you've got to ask yourself one question: 'Do I feel lucky?' Well do ya, punk?"[3]

Eastwood was pointing his huge .44 Smith & Wesson Model 29 revolver at his enemy; several of the bullets were spent. The question was, how many bullets were left. Of course, there was one last bullet that the bad guy got to catch with his body. Every boy in America loved that suspenseful scene. I guess what I'm saying is that "I felt lucky" after the sudden death of John Hurley. It is always a good idea to step back on occasion and feel lucky for what you have and for whom you know and love. Of course, later in life I would learn this lesson again in a deeper, much more dramatic way.

My love of flying started at the age of 14. When I was in the ninth grade, our local civil air patrol held a fundraiser. They raised money by charging people to take a brief flight around the airfield. My dad was kind enough to treat me to a short flight. I must say, that was one of the most exciting experiences of my life, and I knew then, even though I could not express it as such, that I was in love with the pure adrenaline of flight. I joined the civil air patrol. I looked very sharp in my white shirt, navy blue slacks, black shoes, black socks, and my proud cap, poised on the top of my head at an angle. I thought I was hot stuff. It was fun, and we learned a lot. We used to march in cadence. One of the cadences we used to chant went like this:

> M1 caliber 30
> Mighty heavy, mighty dirty!
> Sound off: 1, 2, 3, 4!

Civil air patrol was fun for a while, but I quickly figured out that being in the civil air patrol didn't pay anything. So I eventually left because it interfered with my after school job as a dishwasher at Howley's restaurant.

Just prior to turning 16, I bought my first car. No, my parents did not buy me a car. I saved the money myself. It seems like the kids today are used to the entitlement program and think they deserve a car, and a brand-new one at that. They would rather have things given to them instead of getting a job and earning them. They expect an allowance for the privilege of being born and gracing us with their presence. I think I had more pride in my car because I bought it myself. It wasn't handed to me on a silver platter. Besides, our household silver was in short supply.

Cars are magic to boys. I'm not sure what it is about cars and boys, but I've always believed there is some sort of odd, unexplained connection between the male species and the automobile. Just go to a car show and watch men drooling over shiny new cars or finely restored antiques on the show floor. I don't know what it is, but maybe testosterone creates a magnetic force that is attracted to sheet metal. I worked hard and saved my money, and the first car I bought was a beauty. As they say, beauty is in the eye of the beholder. I thought it was beautiful, but I don't think many other people did. It was a fixer-upper: a 1970 red Datsun 2000 two-seat convertible roadster.

Because the car needed a lot of repair, I was able to buy it for only $800. I say that it was red, but that is a huge exaggeration—it had actually been sun bleached to a depressing, dull maroon. The starter was broken, but I was resourceful, and it could easily be push started because the car was a manual five speed. I had to take action; a guy has to have his wheels!

I recruited my Dad to help. We had tools, and we liked to work on cars together, so we installed a rebuilt starter. My dad borrowed my car one day to drive to work when his car was in the shop. When he was returning home, he accidentally ran into the back of a truck and put a small dent in the front. This turned out to be a stroke of luck. I then took a body-shop-and-paint class at the local tech school in the evening. I prepared and painted my beloved roadster a beautiful glossy white, a nice contrast to its black interior. I would drive with the top down, with two surfboards in the backseat standing up like fins, and everybody could see that I was "styling and profiling"!

You would think that my next car would have been one that was more modern, but I actually shopped in the other direction. At the age of 17, I sold the Datsun 2000, and I bought my next fixer-upper: a 1945 Willys sedan delivery Jeep. It was a panel wagon painted blue with white wheels on the rear. That wagon was the coolest set of wheels ever. It was a panel truck with wide tires and rims on the rear. Much to my delight, the engine had already been changed to a Chevy 283 small-block V-8, and it had a three-speed manual transmission. The door panels had a lot of corrosion and rust, and I needed to repair the paint.

My dad and I went to an auto-body class and used my wagon as a project. It took a little while to complete, but we painted it a beautiful brown color with Imron polyurethane metallic flake paint. I cut out the middle of the roof to install an air vent scoop so that the backseat would be cooled down while driving. I took it to a vinyl top shop, and they installed yellow vinyl on the roof portion of the wagon. I changed the transmission to a racing four-speed Muncie with a racing Hurst shifter. I painted the interior of the engine compartment, painted the Chevy engine with blaze orange paint, and put gold Moroso valve covers on. Yes, I was a gear head! Let me tell you, that was a hot rod! I was retro before retro was cool. Thinking back on it, it was one of my favorite rides.

After class in high school, I would often go to a barren beach between Lake Worth and Lantana to study on my beach towel. That way I would be studying in a place that I loved, instead of in a stuffy, old library. One day, after studying for an hour, I took a walk down the beach. About several hundred yards down, I was shocked to see *a body* lying lifeless in the sand. Have you ever seen a camera zoom quickly in a movie when a character spots something? That's how the scene laid out for me.

I was in a sheer panic. There was a beautiful, blonde teenage girl lying in the sand right at the surf line. The mermaid wasn't moving, and she looked…well, she looked like she was dead. I hoped that she wasn't. I went over to check on her and shook her shoulder a few times, and she didn't respond. I noticed she was breathing, but unconscious. I missed out on the opportunity to perform mouth-to-mouth resuscitation! I scooped her up in my arms and carried her about 100 yards to the first condominium I saw to the south. I climbed the stairs with her and gently laid her down on a chaise lounge. She lay there in her bright yellow bathing suit, coated with sand, looking like she was taking a nap. The condo residents spotted me and called the paramedics right away. The paramedics arrived, checked her vitals, and whisked her off to JFK hospital with the sirens blaring.

As I stood watching the ambulance disappear into the horizon, I hoped that I had saved her and that she would be OK. Before leaving, the paramedics said they would take her to JFK hospital in Lantana and offered to meet me there. I was incredibly curious to find out what happened to the "mystery blonde." After hustling back down the beach to my hot rod Willys, I drove to the hospital. The blonde beauty had regained consciousness, and I was able to speak to her. She had tried to take a long walk on the hot beach and passed out from dehydration. The paramedics told her this "fine young gentleman" (me) had found her unconscious on the beach and carried her to a condo complex nearby. When I met her, she thanked me endlessly for rescuing her. She knew that with evening approaching, she probably would have died right there on the beach if I had not found her lying in the sand. Maybe I saved her; she certainly thought so. In fact, I guess I was her hero.

For the first time in my life, I had done a significant good deed, something really special, and it felt good. She was very interested in becoming more than friends, and I guess I had made a favorable impression on our unofficial first date, but alas I was already dating another gorgeous blonde named Pat. Drat! Even though the opportunity seemed too good to be true, I always had a sense of right and wrong and was loyal to Pat. Just my luck! The one time I saved somebody's life and I rescued a beautiful damsel in distress, I was already committed to someone else. Sigh. I can't remember her name, but I'll always have a Polaroid snapshot in my head of her lying in the sand like a beautiful, washed-up mermaid that had come ashore. I sometimes wonder where she is now and if she remembers that day.

When I became a senior in high school, my full-time summer job as a landscape engineer ended. I needed an after-school, part-time job so I asked my father for some ideas. He scratched his head for a moment and said, "Well, why don't you go down to the local airport and see if you can find a job there?" He had heard that there were kids working for airlines handling baggage on the ramps. I thought this was a great idea, because I had always loved planes and flying.

After inquiring at all of the airlines, they directed me to Aircraft Services Incorporated, which had the baggage handling contracts with United and National airlines. Because of my charm and good looks (or maybe because I was lucky) I was hired to handle the baggage, dump the lavatories, and clean the cabins. Occasionally, I would even get to meet the pilots wearing their dapper pilot uniforms and get to look into the cockpit. I was amazed by a whole new world of dials, gauges, switches, throttles, and flight controls. I knew then that the cockpit was where I wanted to be. I wanted to fly, and I knew it in every fiber of my being.

While I was still a senior in high school, I researched the local college and I found out they had a two-year AS degree program in aerospace technology.

What's funny is on occasion I would attend parties where my friends were all smoking marijuana, which was fairly common at the time. I wasn't a saint, and I wasn't a sinner, but I often took my friends up on their offer to smoke some grass when we were at parties. Ironically, what got me out of smoking marijuana was flying. So I traded the gentle high of marijuana for the incredible high of flying. Flying, in many ways, saved me.

Do you remember the junkie that I told you about before? Kevin popped in and out when he needed another heroin fix. Well, when I was around 18, he popped in again and conned my parents out of $20. He asked if he could come back to sleep on our couch after meeting with some friends. I knew exactly what he had scammed the money for, so I waited up for him. It was after midnight, and we did not lock our doors in those days. All of the lights were off as I sat in the corner of the living room in a floral-patterned swivel chair, gripping my Louisville Slugger baseball bat very tightly. I stood up to greet him. He was as high as a kite with bloodshot eyes. He knew that I was ready to take some serious action. I told him to leave and that he would meet his maker if he ever tried to take advantage of my parents' good nature again. I never told anyone about this event, as he took me seriously and was gone forever from our lives. I was a young man then, and I was a protector of my family!

After graduating from high school, I was able to keep my job at Aircraft Services while going to college, which helped me pay for tuition and flying lessons. Later that year, my dad suggested talking to Imperial Aviation about a job as a loadmaster. I was very stunned when they hired me! How cool was that? I was going to college, taking flying lessons in a Cessna 150, and flying as a crewmember on a Fairchild Hiller 227 cargo-and-passenger plane. This plane was a big, white beautiful bird with a blue stripe. I started out as a full-time employee at Imperial, and they paid me $800 a month. When I was not in school or flying as a loadmaster, I would work on the airplane at night, cleaning, servicing, and doing light mechanical jobs.

On cargo flights, the first officer would let me take his seat to fly the airplane. I was thrilled. When I went for my private license, I not only had experience flying the Cessna 150 flying time, but I also had eight hours of instruction in the multi-engine Fairchild Hiller 227!

On the ground, I enjoyed the Willys for a few years. One day I was driving home after a day of flying back from the Bahamas. A car full of young men pulled out right in front of me and caught my right front bumper. The Willys was top-heavy, and it rolled over onto the driver side, where I had just been leaning my left arm. If I had not pulled in my arm quickly, it would have been crushed under the rolling jeep. There was crashing, banging, and sparks flying everywhere. I thought the Willys was going to explode, so I jumped out through the open passenger window and ran for dear life. Maybe I had seen too many movies where cars exploded on impact.

The young man's insurance company was nice enough to pay me $5,500 because the jeep was totaled. I originally paid $800 for the jeep and had put a few bucks into it with a lot of sweat equity. That really paid off. As it turns out, my next fixer-upper was a 1972 Porsche 914. It was missing the fourth gear, so I got the seller down to $2,000 and spent $400 to repair it. I was able to bank some nice money. Talk about trading up!

Flying to the Bahamas was awesome for me! We got to eat at the officers' mess hall, and we stayed in the officers' barracks when we stayed on the weekends. They also had helicopters that flew logistics to other smaller stations down the island of Andros. Occasionally, I would get to ride on some of these trips. I was able to get my private pilot's license not long after that.

My job for Imperial Aviation was a great position because I was upgraded to first officer after getting my commercial instrument and multi-engine ratings with about 600 hours of flight time. I was offered the first officer position because another pilot left Imperial Aviation for a better job with America West Airlines, and I had experience flying the Fairchild Hiller 227. At the time, Imperial Aviation paid their first officers $1,200 a month. That was extremely awesome for a fresh, new pilot. I was thrilled with the progress I was making and so excited to be doing what I loved. I loved what I was doing.

When I was 20, I graduated from Palm Beach Junior College as a first officer. Life was very, very good. I enrolled in the Embry-Riddle Aeronautical University extension program for aviation administration. I had plenty of time to study on flights and on weekends in the Bahamas. Being a water lover, I enjoyed snorkeling in the beautiful waters full of tropical fish.

Later that year, I went for a ride with my friend Scott in his dad's Boeing Stearman. The Stearman is an open cockpit bi-plane, and it was a wild ride. He looped, rolled, and flew inverted until the fuel ran out of the carburetor, and then he flipped it upright and the engine came back to life. That hooked me. I had to have my own aerobatic flying plane!

I borrowed a few bucks from my dad and grandma and combined that with my own savings to buy a Bellanca Citabria. It was the least expensive aerobatic airplane available. It was a tail dragger, tandem seater (one seat in front and one in the rear), with a control joystick coming out of the floor. Owning your own plane is expensive, so I figured out a scheme to help pay for the plane. I did wing walking. OK, just kidding. What I really did is rent out my Bellanca Citabria airplane through the Chandelle flying club. That revenue helped pay for maintenance and tie-down fees. The gentleman who ran the club was a former Army pilot with aerobatic experience. He taught me the basics. After reading and studying different aerobatic books, I learned to become proficient at loops, rolls, Cuban eights, and hammerheads. It was great to take my family and friends up and turn them inside out and upside down. My friend Ed actually lost his lunch on one of those flights. Fortunately he didn't lose it on my neck!

With about 1500 hours of recorded flying time and two years experience as a first officer on a FH-227 plane, I applied to BizJet, a Learjet Management and Charter company, and was hired there as a first officer. Flying on a Learjet was a ride!

The Learjet was originally designed as a fighter-bomber for the Swedish Air Force. After a year with BizJet, I was allowed to take my Airline Transportation Rating with a type rating. Captains are required to have a type rating to fly any aircraft that weighs over 12,500 pounds. So now I was, as they say, in the catbird seat.

At 23 years old, I was flying a Learjet as a captain. Joe Townsend—who came from humble beginnings—was now a captain and was flying millionaires like Jimmy Buffet around the country in a little rocket plane.

Sweet!

What was really amazing about Joe's later teen years and young adult years was that anything seemed possible. He is a person who came from humble beginnings. But the word *no* didn't seem to be in his vocabulary. *Is that part of it?* I thought. *Is it the people who have next to nothing who work harder to make something of their life? Maybe they appreciate it more because they aren't handed things and they have to work for them?* I thought about it.

He owned his own plane at a young age and became a Leerjet captain at a very young age. Joe seemed to take advantage of every minute, and he lived life to the fullest each and every day.

I wonder if it was the sense of mortality he learned by losing friends. He just seemed to always be having fun on a wild adventure ride called life. How many people don't? How many people just give up and take the safe road in life when they could be so much more? How many people view their lives as a series of tasks instead of an adventure? To me, that is an important lesson Joe can teach us as we look at his late teen years. The other irony that hit me was that flying was the joy of his life and saved him in many ways, but later in life would be the source of near destruction. Joe seemed to be telling us that we have to take those risks in order to get the rewards—that nothing worth anything in life doesn't have a risk involved. That is a brave lesson.

"Joe, that was a great story. It sounds like you had a lot of fun, but I need to know how you met Kelley and all that," I said, after listening to Joe's stories about his teen years.

"Well, Buddy, I would be glad to you more about my angels," he replied.

"Why don't you give me a call next Monday or Tuesday night. I will be in Ohio doing training," I said.

"OK; that sounds good. I will call you next week," said Joe.

"That is a 10-4, Captain," I replied.

"OK, let's get the correct lingo. We're not talking on a CB radio. Flying lingo might be, 'Roger that,'" Joe explained.

"OK, Roger that, Captain!" I responded.

ENDNOTES

1. Orison Swett Marden, quoted in *Quotations Book;* http://quotationsbook.com/quote/18068/; accessed May 18, 2011.

2. Terri Gulick, quoted on *Brain Dash;* http://www.braindash.com/quotes/terri_gulick/if_its_meant_to_be_its_up_to_me/; accessed May 18, 2011.

3. "Dirty Harry (1971)—Memorable Quotes," *The Internet Movie Database;* http://www.imdb.com/title/tt0066999/quotes; accessed May 19, 2011.

Chapter 4

The Townsend Girls

I love you not only for what you are, but for what I am when I am
with you. I love you not only for what you have made of yourself,
but for what you are making of me. I love you for the part
of me that you bring out.—Roy Croft[1]

I got off my plane in Ohio and rolled my luggage along to the rental car pickup area. I picked up my car and drove to the hotel, checked in, and went to my room where I dropped my luggage on the floor. I stretched out on the bed and let out a long sigh. I have always loved hotels. I don't know why, but maybe it's the idea that you have finally reached your destination and it is time to relax a bit.

I knew Joe would be calling later. On my trip I had opened the file of newspaper clippings and other photos Joe had sent me of old articles about the crash. The newsprint was starting to yellow and curl on the edges. Grainy newsprint pictures of Joe with his daughter in the cockpit of a plane, the family photo, pictures of three white coffins lined up at the funeral. Those pictures really had me thinking. They are from another time, but they brought back for me the soul-bleaching sadness, the enormous loss that Joe faced and lives with every day. How? He is always cheerful, always upbeat, and always cracking jokes about everything. It got me thinking about my life and how I have dealt with adversity. It got me thinking of people who whine about all sorts of life's little inconveniences, but don't realize how lucky they are. I guess it is human nature to take the small things and even the big things for granted. Until we lose them. Only then do we mourn the loss of what once was, and wish we had it back.

Just then my cell phone started to vibrate on top of the dresser, dancing and playing its nifty little tune.

I picked up the phone. "Hello?"

"Hey, Shawnee, this is your buddy, Joseppy."

"Greetings, Captain Joseppy! How are you?"

"I am doing wonderfully well, Shawn. I just got back this weekend from attending a truck rally in Colorado Springs. The kind of truck I drive is not your ordinary truck. It is called a Super Sport Roadster (SSR), built by Chevrolet from 2003 until 2006. I met a lot of cool people and saw a lot of cool SSR trucks. The best day was when I got to lead the cruise up to the Royal Gorge in my Sling Shot Yellow SSR with another 47 SSRs on the bridge at one time. It is a 1,000 foot drop below the bridge to a magnificent canyon and the Arkansas River," Joseph explained.

"That's great," I said. "Glad you enjoyed yourself. So what's up, Captain?"

"Well, last time we talked you said you wanted to hear the story of my years with Kelley and the girls and how our branch of the Townsend family tree got started. Well, maybe it's a trunk and not a branch," he said chuckling.

"Yes, that is true, Joe. Tell you what, if tonight is good for you, let me grab a quick sandwich, and I will call you back in an hour. How does that sound, Joe?"

"That sounds fabulous, Shawn. Talk to you soon."

I rang him about an hour later.

"Hey, Joe, this is Shawn. Is it still a good time to talk?" I asked.

"Absolutely. It's a great time to talk. So where were we anyway?" Joe replied.

"Well," I said, "the last thing I remember is that you were flitting around the country in some little rocket plane."

"Yep. That's right," Joe said. "I'll pick up the story from there."

"OK. Sounds good," I replied.

I first met Kelley in high school, even though she was two years younger than I was. She got my attention because she was really cute; she had beautiful, auburn hair and a figure with curves in all the right places from top to bottom. Yes, looks were important, but she had something more; she was the sweetest and friendliest gal you could ever meet, and that made her even more attractive. Everybody liked Kelley. Since she was two years younger than me, we stayed friends while we were in high school. I went off to college and started flying, and we saw each other frequently as friends. We would occasionally go to movies together when I had free time from school or flying.

Some people say that you know the exact moment you go from being a friend to being in love. And I know exactly when that moment was. When you ask people who are in love, they never describe anything complicated;

the love connection is often made in a simple moment. The morning of Kelley's prom, I borrowed a Cadillac Seville from my parents friends. I took it over to Kelley's home, as I thought it would be fun if we washed the car together. We were being silly, playing around with each other and spraying water. The weather was perfect, and I looked at Kelley and knew that I was in love and that I would eventually marry her.

For the prom, she wore a long form-fitting gown that was glamorous, but not ostentatious. That was always her style—simple, yet elegant. The prom was held at the incredibly beautiful Henry Morrison Flagler Museum in Palm Beach, a huge 60,000 square foot mansion that Henry built for his wife in 1902.

After I began flying Learjets and was making enough money to support a family, we got truly serious and began a loving relationship. I knew that I was in love because Kelley was constantly in my thoughts. When I was 21, I went out and bought a huge cardboard box at Christmas time. I wanted Kelley to have a unique memory for the present I was about to give her. I took that huge box and packed it with all kinds of old pots, pans, coffee percolators, and other household items. In the middle of all of that junk, I placed the engagement ring inside the percolator that was sitting at the bottom of the box.

When she opened the Christmas gift, I told her that it was the start of our new home together, all in one box. She was smart enough to know that there must be a small box in there somewhere, so she dug into the box until she got to the old percolator and found the box with the diamond engagement ring. She was so excited and had tears of joy in her eyes, knowing that someday we would be man and wife. We did not set a date, but we continued dating seriously and falling in love. I wish I could say that the story ended there, but because I hadn't grown up yet, it wasn't the fairytale ending that one would hope for.

Eventually, as the wedding plans started and we did the blood test and talked about the marriage certificate, I got a disease that affects the circulation in the lower extremities, which is medically known as *cold feet*.

I don't know why I got scared of the commitment. Maybe I was just too young. I asked if we could wait longer before setting a date to get married, and that did not go over very well. But Kelley was very patient. We stayed friends, and we still hung out, and she waited. She was a very patient person, maybe more patient than I deserved at the time.

Then a defining moment happened. Piedmont Airlines hired me as a flight engineer, and I moved to Virginia Beach. The old saying that "Absence makes the heart grow fonder" must surely be true, because being so far away from Kelley made me miss her like crazy. When you miss someone, the phone calls and the postcards try to fill the cracks in your loneliness, but nothing seems to help.

I realized I truly loved Kelley and I missed her. I took a trip back to West Palm Beach and took Kelley to dinner. We dined at Chuck and Harold's in Palm Beach on Royal Poinciana Way, a beautiful road lined with tall, elegant Royal Palm trees. After dinner I took her hand and told her that I loved her and was ready to spend the rest of my life with her. For some reason, she actually accepted, and we scheduled our wedding for July 6, 1985. The good news is that Kelley had never returned the ring, and she was able to wear it again.

We got married on July 6, 1985. I remember that Kelley was wearing a beautiful, white, tea-length wedding dress. It was a hot July day in Florida, and she looked calm, cool, and crisp. I was wearing a white tux with tails and was feeling a tremendous sense of happiness. It was, in every sense of the word, a traditional wedding complete with the wedding march and 250 of our closest friends and family. The pastor was Brother Joe Ranieri, a friend of my family's. He was not a priest, just a brother that could marry us. My dad was delighted to be my best man, and I was delighted to have him as my best man. The maid of honor was a very close friend of Kelley's, Schotzi Oenbrink. She was a real character. Sadly, she passed away several years after we married due to a brain aneurysm. She left behind three small children and her husband. After that, Kelley and I talked about our own mortality, and she made me promise to remarry if anything ever happened to her.

The reception was at the West Palm Beach Elks Lodge, and they also did the catering. It wasn't a fancy wedding in any sense of the word, but we were not really into fancy; we were just into having a good time and being around friends and family. Finally, Kelley was mine.

A close friend of Kelley's named Kelly Coyle worked at the amazingly beautiful Breakers Hotel in Palm Beach. For a wedding gift, she was able to arrange one night for us in a beachfront room. On our wedding night, I carried my new bride across the threshold. We turned the air conditioning up so that it got as cold as it could get, and we opened up the sliding glass doors to the balcony so we could hear the crashing surf on the beach. It was a beautiful evening and a fine way to start our new life together.

The rest of the honeymoon was not very glamorous; it was spent packing up all of Kelley's belongings and her cat Blossom into her grandfather's black Ford F-150 pickup truck. She moved to Virginia Beach to share a life with me. I had bought a 2 bedroom, 2 1/2 baths, single garage townhome. Our backyard overlooked the Lynn Haven River in Virginia Beach. It was very picturesque, with a beautiful wood deck, and it was at the end of a cul-de-sac. The entrance of the development was marked with a ceremonial totem pole. We had a wood-burning fireplace, so we bought a cord of wood, which lasted a long time. On many chilly nights, we spent time snuggling in front of a crackling fire and enjoying being man and woman. I don't know why, but staring into a crackling fire is hypnotic. We were a very happy young married couple.

We took our real honeymoon later on to Sarajevo, Yugoslavia. Yep, that's right—not Niagara Falls, the Poconos, or some tropical island, but Yugoslavia. If we were going to honeymoon, I wanted the honeymoon to be first class. We went to Yugoslavia to snow ski.

Kelley had only skied once before in Massanutten, Virginia, with me. She took a lesson and we met up later to go skiing together. It was probably too early for that, because as we went down the hill, Kelley was not turning to slow down; her skis were pointed straight down the mountain. It did not take long for her to reach warp speed and to start flying down the hill at a zillion miles an hour, screaming at the top of her lungs in sheer terror. I tried to catch up with her, but she was already gone. Finally, at the bottom of the hill, she fell over. I found her in a pile of crumpled skis and poles. That was enough of that, so we drove back to our home.

Because of Kelley's fresh memory of that terrifying event, I decided she needed more ski lessons. At that time, you could get a lot for your dollar in Sarajevo, so I signed Kelley up to get private lessons from a blonde, buff, ski instructor, and she learned to ski quite well. The entire honeymoon was wonderful, as we got to stay in the resort chalet on the mountain with breakfast and dinner included every day. One night, the resort had a pig roast and two waiters carried a huge pig on a spit on their shoulders and the staff followed them in a Congo line. A waiter lit a cigarette and put it in the pig's mouth so that the pig looked like he was smoking when they carried it around. Maybe that's where smoked meat comes from! All in all, it was a wonderful honeymoon and we headed home after a grand time.

After being married for a few years, Kelley and I moved back to West Palm Beach. At first, we alternated staying with her parents or with my sister Rose. We looked at several houses and finally found a lot on a water-ski lake. We decided to build our own home there for our future. To save money, I acted as the contractor. I got the building permits as an owner-builder and took care of the land. I installed all the low-voltage wiring, did the painting, landscaping, and lots of cleanup. When the house was ready, we moved into our new home and got ready to build a family.

We had been married for four years at this point, and we were ready to have children, which is often the next step for young couples in love. It's funny what we sometimes take for granted and what fools us by not happening. We tried everything to have a baby. We practiced a lot. Kelly was charting her cycle, taking her temperature, marking calendars, and doing all the things that experts say to do. We were one giant biology laboratory.

If I was going to be on a trip during the "forecasted" fertility time, Kelley would either fly with me or meet me at my destination—and then…nothing. Nada. Zilch. So it was time to do some testing. Kelley's doctor was ready to run tests on us. My test was, of course, the easiest one to give first, and they discovered that there were lots of happy swimmers in my pool.

Kelley did not have it quite so easy. She had to undergo a laparoscopic procedure before being put on special medications. Her doctor found some blockages in her tubes and cleared them up. Then a miracle happened: boom! Finally, after three years of trying, we were pregnant the very next month after Kelley's procedure. Kelley was pregnant with our first child, Laura Lee.

Around the same time, I joined the Shriners' Flying Fez unit. Although this sounds like a big, red, fuzzy blimp, the Flying Fez unit is a group of pilots who fly uninsured children from low-income families to Shriners' hospitals for treatment. It is a very rewarding and meaningful mission to be a part of.

In late April of 1992, Kelly was already two weeks late. She was feeling fine, and the pregnancy had been problem free. I received word that there were two children who needed to be flown to a Shriners hospital in Pensacola, Florida. I asked her gently if she thought it would be OK. "Oh, sure," she said. "I am feeling great, and these kids really need to be taken care of. Besides, Joe, I'm not having any contractions." Given Kelley's reassurance, a friend and I flew two children in a twin Bonanza plane to Pensacola, which was a three-hour flight each way.

When I arrived, I called Kelley using a pay phone (there were no cell phones back then), and she told me that the contractions had just started. I could have taken a flight home on a commercial airliner or flown the twin-engine Bonanza back and been home in only a couple of hours, but Kelley told me not to. Kelley responded, "No. Fly the kids back to West Palm once they have seen their doctors." The next day, Kelley went into labor, and we went to the birthing center at St. Mary's Hospital. Our beautiful little Laura Lee was born on a bright, sunny afternoon. My sister, Mary

Anne, was a delivery nurse at St. Mary's, so she was right there with us all the way. It was a wonderful feeling to be a dad and to be able to share the birth of a new life with both my wife and my sister.

Kelley was a fantastic mother and wife. When she was pregnant, she read all sorts of books about babies and how to care for herself and the baby after the baby was born. She loved to cook and clean and always kept a wonderful home. The greatest thing about Kelley was that she was a consummate optimist; she was always happy, always upbeat, and always ready to do something fun together. This is why she attracted friends to her like a magnet. She loved to sail with friends on a Hobie Cat (a small, twin-hulled sailboat). Kelley radiated warmth. She loved people, and people loved her back. In a sense, Kelley was love.

Tara Nicole followed not too far after her big sister and was born in May of 1995. I don't know why, but both of our kids were late for their own birth. Tara was about two weeks late, and we had her at the same St. Mary's Hospital where we had Laura Lee. Kelley was only 5 foot 2 inches tall and a very petite woman, so labor was always very hard work for her. I was the dutiful coach with the ice chips and the cool washcloth and had gone to class with her to practice breathing. We were very blessed that both of our children were born healthy with nice sets of lungs to cry when they got their bottoms swatted. I don't think I've ever heard a more charming sound than a baby's first cry.

I remember when Laura Lee was about a month old, she was crying her eyes out one evening, with giant, alligator tears falling down her cute little face. Kelley was pulling her hair out because, no matter what she did, Laura would not stop crying. I scooped up Laura in my arms and carried her outside to give Kelley a break. It was a beautiful evening with an ink-black blanket of sky punctuated by bright, pinpoint stars. As soon as we were outside, Laura started cuddling in my arms as she stared up at the sky; she was totally at peace. You might say it was a Kodak moment. It was very rare that Laura or Tara ever cried for more than a few minutes, and they were loved back with either a soothing diaper change or some of mama's milk.

Laura Lee was quite the energetic little imp. She wanted to be in gymnastics at the age of three and did really well, amazing both her mom and me. She loved the rolling and tumbling and jumping and all the daredevil moves that gymnastics has. She starred in the Cinderella show at the age of four as the bluebird. Both Laura Lee and Tara (who we also liked to call "Tara Bug") loved Barney. They loved to see Barney. They loved to watch Barney. They loved to sing with Barney, dance with Barney, and convince their dad to buy Barney products. In case you have lived in a cave somewhere for the last two decades, Barney is a silly purple dinosaur on a children's television show who has a very goofy voice and laugh.

A friend of ours, Bob Bentz, had a birthday party for his daughter, and Barney made a guest appearance. Surprisingly, his daughters were scared to death of this giant, purple dinosaur. Not Laura Lee; she was all over that big, purple dinosaur. It was a hug-a-thon. She was in love and gave Barney lots of love and kisses. So, of course, later in the year we had a combined birthday party for Laura and Tara and invited Barney and Baby Bop to be the guests of honor. Kids were in the pool, jumping in the bounce house, hanging out by the snow-cone machine, and eating cake. Where was Laura Lee? She was making moon eyes over and hugging her pal Barney. There were about a hundred kids and parents there and everybody had a fabulous time.

I'm sure you have heard the saying, "The apple does not fall far from the tree." I guess it must be true. Most infants and toddlers are terrified of fireworks because they are very loud and very bright. Those loud booms scare the daylights out of most little kids. Not ours. Both Laura and Tara loved firework shows with loud booms as infants. They loved going to air shows. One would sit on my shoulders as I carried the other, while screaming fighter jets roared by just over our heads. They would stare up into the sky laughing, smiling, and pointing. I guess all Townsends love adrenaline!

When Laura Lee was around three years old, we went to a church carnival with rides. It was a typical local carnival that travels around the country. She and I went on the Ferris Wheel together, and she loved it. When the South Florida fair was in town, we went on other fast, daring rides, and she loved them as well. Nothing could scare this kid. She definitely would have been a daredevil like her daddy.

In December of 1994, Kelley, Laura Lee, and I went skiing in Breckenridge Colorado. Laura Lee was two-and-a-half years old and, as I was an accomplished skier, Laura rode on my back in a backpack designed for toddlers. She laughed, giggled, and loved every minute of it. She was our little snow bunny.

When I was returning home from an airline trip, Laura Lee was the first to come racing down the hallway into my arms yelling, "Daddy! Daddy! Daddy! Daddy!" Tara Bug, her little sister, would come waddling up behind her, and I would scoop them both up into my arms and give them a big family hug. Kelley would follow the babies, and we would have a second family hug all together. It became our Dad-is-home-from-a-flying-trip ritual.

For Christmas in 1994, we bought Laura Lee a BB gun as she wanted to follow in dad's footsteps and become an avid hunter. After teaching her safety, how to work the trigger, and some shooting techniques, we would practice target shooting into a cardboard box. Soon, she became a pretty good little shot; she was my little Annie Oakley. One day, there was a water snake on the lift in the boathouse. Laura Lee was insistent that she wanted to give it a shot, finally having some live prey to practice on. Believe it or not, Laura hit that snake right between its beady little eyes on the first shot.

The girls also had a bright pink Barbie Jeep. (What other color would it be?) Laura Lee was the driver, and Tara rode as the dutiful passenger. They would climb in the little car and have a great time trying to run me over as I taunted them in the driveway. I was very fast and agile. Just as they were about to hit me, I would suddenly lift my leg over their heads and jump as the car passed underneath me, which, of course, created a chorus of giggles and laughs.

Laura Lee started pre-kindergarten at the tender age of three years old. She was cute and lovable and made lots of friends there. One day, I was asked to come in my pilot's uniform to talk to the children about what I did for my job. At the time, the airline used to give away little stick-on wings for children, and I brought enough for each kid to have their own set of wings. I also helped chaperone one of Laura Lee's field trips to a local citrus grove where, for some strange reason, there was an alligator wrestler. (Well, it was Florida after all.) I carried Laura Lee on my shoulders as a proud daddy so she could see the show put on by the alligator wrestler.

When Tara Nicole was a toddler, she figured out pretty quickly that when the refrigerator door opened, food was not far behind. So whenever Kelley or I would go into the kitchen and open the refrigerator door, Tara Nicole would come waddling up looking for a treat. What was even more humorous was that she was not yet speaking. She would just grunt and point, hoping that we would get the message that she was sending, which was, "I sure would like a treat from that big metal thing!" We nicknamed her "Tara Bug" because she was the cutest little toddler who ever was.

On the evenings I was home, Kelley would prepare dinner, and I would take the girls in a bike trailer for a ride around the block, always stopping at our favorite bench at the end of the lake and then continuing on to the playground. They always loved that little trip around the neighborhood. That's the funny thing about young children. To a young child, everything is a fascinating adventure. After dinner, we would often watch television on their little couch. When Laura got tired, she would drink from her bottle, her arm wrapped under my chin and holding onto my earlobe until she fell fast asleep. I always thought that it was an odd little quirk to hold my earlobe, but it sure was so cute. You know when you are a father, and you love your little daughter so deeply, you cherish those kinds of moments.

It will come as no surprise to you that the girls also loved the trampoline. I would jump with them in my arms, one at a time when they were young. On the trampoline Laura loved playing "Duck, duck, goose." We would always let her win.

In the house, the girls loved playing "London Bridge is Falling Down" and they would always giggle really loudly when the bridge fell and I caught them. We used to play the Hokey Pokey song and they loved to dance to that:

> You put your right foot in,
> You put your right foot out,
> You put your right foot in,
> And you shake it all about.
> You do the Hokey Pokey
> And you turn yourself around.
> That's what it's all about!

I would often watch videos with Laura and Tara on the little couch. They would watch Barney, Cinderella, the Lion King, Winnie the Pooh, and other typical small-child fare. Winnie the Pooh was one of my favorites; I could definitely relate to Tigger. Tigger was always happy and optimistic about his day—always, no matter what happened. The essential quality of Tigger is in me, and I believe it has always been in me. I was a Tigger before Tigger! I would often sing the Tigger song with my girls:

> A wonderful thing is a Tigger,
> A Tigger's a wonderful thing.
> Their tops are made out of rubber,
> Their bottoms are made out of spring.
> Their bouncy, bouncy, bouncy, bouncy,
> Fun, fun, fun, fun, fun!
> The most wonderful thing
> about Tiggers is:
> I'm the only one![2]

Believe it or not, on one flying trip, my first officer had little children, and we talked about our favorite kids shows. Next thing I knew, I found myself singing the Tigger song in the cockpit with another dad. I guess I really am Tigger!

When in town, I would ski sometimes twice each day. In the mornings either Kelley or my buddy Joey would pull me behind our ski boat on the lake behind our home. If it was Kelley driving, we strapped both the babies into the bench seat. They were able to watch Daddy cutting up the slalom ski course, until the rope was shortened too much, and then they would see daddy doing a spectacular, funny wipeout. They always liked that.

"Well, Shawn, it's getting late and I know you have a big day tomorrow," Joe concluded.

"Yeah, you are right. I gotta go," I said, realizing the time. "Joe?" I said.

"Yeah?" he replied.

"Thanks for sharing your family with me. I wish I could have met them," I said warmly.

"Someday you will…in another place," Joe said.

"Yes. Good night, Joe," I replied.

"Night," Joe said as he hung up the phone.

Endnotes

1. This is Roy Croft's "modern" translation of an original sonnet by Elizabeth Barrett Browning. Roy Croft, "Wedding Guide Love," *The Family Book of Best Loved Poems,* David L. George, Ed. (Garden City, New York: Doubleday & Company, Inc, 1952).

2. Richard M. Sherman and Robert B. Sherman, "The Wonderful Thing About Tiggers," *The Many Adventures of Winnie the Pooh* (1968).

Chapter 5

King Lear and His Flying Machine

Pursue your passion, and be passionate about what you pursue.
—Joe Townsend

I sat in the cell-phone parking lot at the Philadelphia Airport waiting for Joe to arrive. Joe had called me a few weeks earlier and told me he was flying from Florida to Colorado on US Airways. He offered to stop in Philadelphia for a few hours and have lunch. I agreed that it was a great idea. Our phone conversations had established a foundation for our friendship, and I was looking forward to having lunch with him.

The phone rang on the seat beside me in the car. When I answered, Joe said, "Hey, Shawn. This is Joe. I am here."

"I am on my way," I replied.

I pulled up to the curb alongside the airport terminal, and Joe recognized me right away. He walked quickly over and jumped into the car. We shook hands warmly.

"Gee, Joe," I said, "do you look younger?"

Joe looked at me and smiled. "No, I'm not any younger. I feel pretty young, though."

I don't know why, but I remembered him looking older than me. Although we had spoken by phone several times, this was the first time we had seen each other face-to-face since our first meeting on a flight months earlier. It's funny the tricks your mind can play on you. With everything he had been through, it seemed he should be worse for wear.

"Well, Joe," I said, "you're my guest here in Philadelphia; what would you like to have for lunch?"

"Well, if it's not too much trouble," he answered, "I really would love to have an authentic Philadelphia cheese steak sandwich."

It was chilly that day and too cold to eat outside so I took Joe to the Reading Terminal Market, where there were many places that serve cheese steak sandwiches. It's a charming place in downtown Philadelphia that has been there since the late 1800s.

We got our sandwiches and sat down, grinning at each other like old, fast friends.

"It's good to see you, man," I said.

"Yeah you too, buddy," Joe agreed.

Joe had a root beer in a wax paper cup with a lid on it. He slowly slid the paper wrapper off the straw and, after several tries, was able to insert the straw into the slot in the lid.

"Joe, if you don't mind me asking, is that always difficult for you?" I asked.

"No. I don't mind you asking," Joe replied. "It's a condition that I have with my eyes—it was a brain injury from the crash. So when I look at this cup, it is vibrating, and I have to figure out which image is real."

This was a defining moment for me in my understanding of Joe as a person. I felt humbled and inspired as I watched Joe fumble with his straw. I had no idea so many small things were a struggle for Joe in the smallest ways. Yet, Joe was daily choosing to be one who overcomes obstacles. He never complains. I noticed he didn't ask me to help him with it. Nope. He wants to be self-sufficient, and if it takes a few tries to hit the hole in the lid, so what? It wasn't about how many swings it took; it was about just hitting the ball eventually. It's called dogged persistence, and it is a quality in Joe I greatly admire.

"So, Joe," I said, "I really would like to hear the rest of the story. I now feel like I know a lot about your childhood and your teen years, and I feel like I've gotten to know Kelley with the girls. What I really don't know as much about is the history of your flying. I'm fascinated how you so quickly went from flying a 44-seat passenger and cargo planes to Learjets. But I'm sure you have lots of interesting stories about your flying adventures."

"Oh, yes, it was a fun time for sure!"

"Well, I'm going to eat my cheese steak now, and you fill me in because I'm all ears."

Even though we were surrounded by the hustle and bustle of the marketplace, with people walking around and merchants selling their wares, as soon as Joe started talking, everything disappeared. There were no distractions. I was enthralled with Joe's life story.

When I was 22 years old, BizJet hired me as a first officer to fly Learjet models 24, 25, and 35. I guess the best way to describe these jets is to say that they look like a rocket with wings. They were white, long and skinny, and had dramatic blue swooping stripes running down the side of the jet. These jets looked as if speed had been shaped into metal. The 24 was a classic—it was older and had a smaller, beautiful cabin inside with leather seats for the passengers. You always knew, however, that you were sitting in a tube that was going to be taking off like a banshee down the runway. Later, BizJet acquired a Cessna Citation private jet, and I was one of the captains that flew it all hours of the day and night on air-ambulance trips.

Learjets 24 and 25 had a straight turbojet engine that felt like raw power. When full throttle was applied at takeoff, you could hear the engines roaring even on the inside of the plane; you could hear the distinct crackling sound an engine makes when it's roaring. The power in these engines would pin me back in my seat. Do you remember those old stereo ads that showed a guy pinned back in his seat from the blast of sound coming from the stereo? It felt like that.

Sometimes I had passengers who wanted to experience a steep climb. Just after lifting off, I would level the plane just above the runway and rapidly increase my speed. Then I would bring the gear and flaps up. When we reached 250 knots, I would pull the stick back to 45° so that the nose of the plane was facing up toward the sky, which makes you feel like you are going straight up into the heavens. Then I would drop down the speed to 160 knots to get out of the steep climb and execute a wingover to keep a positive g-force and lower the nose. A wingover is a roll to either the left or right while in a climb. Of course, I always requested permission from the control tower first. I found that control towers don't like surprises very much. It's better to keep them informed.

BizJet promoted me to captain at 24 years old, and around the same time, I began to pursue an Air Force Reserve pilot opportunity. A good friend of mine from the ramp days at Aircraft Services, Dexter Franklin, had joined the Air Force reserves flying as a flight engineer on a Lockheed C-141. Kelley and I took a vacation to visit Dexter in Charleston, South Carolina, and to meet Air Force Reserve Colonel Hammond. Most reserve pilots came to the program from active duty, but they did allow a civilian in one slot each year. And let me tell you, Joe Townsend wanted that slot. I was salivating when I saw some of the magnificent machines that Air Force pilots got to fly. I was a great candidate. I had two college degrees. I had been a Learjet captain with thousands of hours of flying time, and I had passed the Air Force officers qualification test with flying colors, no pun intended. I was very excited, and it seemed like my dream was finally going to come true.

Then I went for the physical exam at Homestead Air Force Base, which was southwest of Miami. I was, after all, the perfect specimen of health so an exam would be no problem. When they tested my vision I passed with 20/20 vision, but they noticed and measured a slight correction, and I was off by half of a diopter. That sounds very minor, doesn't it? But an Air Force pilot has to have perfect vision when first tested (after training, corrective lenses could be worn). The military Air Force command really wanted me, so they offered me a slot, but it wasn't the slot that I was looking for. They wanted me to be a navigator. That meant no actual flying, so I graciously declined their offer and stuck to the commercial world of flying. To this day, I still wonder what it would be like to fly one of those fighter jets. As the old Rolling Stones song said:

> You can't always get what you want
> You can't always get what you want
> But if you try sometimes you just might find
> You get what you need.[1]

Since I was getting my thrills flying as a Learjet captain, I decided to sell my Citabria as it was getting high on hours and close to some large, costly maintenance. I found an airplane sales guy who would trade my airplane for a brand, spanking new 1982 Nissan 300 ZX sports car. It was white with a beige pin stripe and had a beige leather interior. It had a T-top roof with a removable panel on both the driver and passenger sides so that the car was kind of like a convertible with a bar in the middle of the roof. The instrument panel was digital, which was really awesome.

There was actually a female voice that would talk to me if I left the lights on after the ignition was off. I called the voice Awesome Audrey. That was my very first brand-new car, and it was far from the fixer-uppers that I was familiar with.

I have had many great adventures while flying Learjets. I had the privilege of having Jimmy Buffett, the singer-songwriter, as my passenger. Jimmy Buffett loves to fly, and he is a very nice man. On one occasion, I flew Jimmy into Atlanta for a concert. My copilot and I were invited to the concert, and we rode in a fancy limo. The rest of Jimmy's band was already in Atlanta, so after meeting up with them, we all got into four limos and went whizzing through town to the concert arena. It was cool to meet Fingers Taylor. He is a phenomenal harmonica player, which is why they call him Fingers Taylor. We were in the last limo and running red lights to keep up. We were invited backstage with the band and got to meet Gary Busey, the actor, who was also backstage.

On another trip with Jimmy, I was flying him from Palm Beach International to Tallahassee, Florida, for a dinner event with Governor Bob Graham. My copilot, Mark, was brand-new to our company. Mark was an experienced twin-engine aircraft pilot, but he was in the learning stage of flying jets and flying really fast. That evening after the dinner, we flew Jimmy to his hometown in Mississippi, and the next day we were scheduled to fly to New Orleans. We heard on the news that a space shuttle was being launched the next day and that it was sitting on the airport ramp atop of a B-747. On the way down to New Orleans, we obtained approval from the control tower to fly a low pass along the length of the runway. We got to see the space shuttle sitting piggyback on its travel partner. On that same trip to Jimmy's small hometown in Mississippi, I flew him down the Great Mississippi River at a low, treetop altitude, and he laughed the whole way. He just loved it!

We landed at New Orleans Lakefront Airport, which was the general aviation airport. Jimmy had a limo waiting there for him and asked if we would like to ride downtown with him. We, of course, said, "Yes.

Thank you!" First, the limo driver took us by Jimmy's apartment, and he showed us the inside of his place and gave us a tour. Jimmy started out in New Orleans playing at local clubs. When we left for the evening, I asked Jimmy what kind of food he wanted us to provide the next day on the flight to Aspen. He said "No, boys. Don't worry about that; I'll bring the food." The next day, Jimmy showed up grinning ear to ear with New Orleans seafood, Po Boy sandwiches, and crawfish in hand. An hour into the flight, Jimmy said he was going to serve us, so he came up to the cockpit and brought us sandwiches and crawfish to enjoy. Jimmy is such a down-to-earth and nice guy!

We were flying to Aspen, Colorado, in the middle of the winter. There was a low-cloud ceiling and all inbound aircraft had to fly using an instrument approach. Unfortunately, there were several planes in a holding pattern waiting to land. I realized that we did not have enough fuel to go into the holding pattern, so I elected to land in Grand Junction, Colorado. When you are landing using an instrument approach, you are given vectors to the final approach path, which lines you up with the runway. When we started our approach to land in Grand Junction, I discovered that the glide slope instrument was not working, so I executed a missed approach.

My inexperienced, new copilot was not completely up to speed about faster approach speeds in the Learjet, so I explained to him that we would now fly a localizer approach with letdown points. The localizer approach lines you up with the runway, but does not have a glide path. I told my copilot that we would set different radials off of another fix, which would give us another letdown point. This worked really well as we broke through the clouds at only 400 feet above the ground and went roaring onto the runway, which was directly ahead. By the way, the minimum requirement is 400 feet. It was snowing to beat the band (no pun intended, Jimmy!) when we landed. As we were landing, Jimmy Buffett was kneeling on the floor between us watching the entire drama play out. It was a memorable trip for us all. My copilot gained a great experience and is now a senior captain with Delta Airlines.

One of the things that Jimmy loved to do was to fly very fast at a low altitude in the Learjet. As the captain, I got a kick out of making him happy. On a flight to St. Martin, he asked me if we could buzz the bay and his home that sat on the hilltop at St. Bart's. I was the captain and my good friend, Joey Piazza, was my first officer. We came in screaming across the sky right above the tops of the sailboat masts in the bay. I was flying right on top of the water and I can only imagine that the Learjet generated a rooster tail in the water like the ones that trail speedboats. When reaching the rising terrain, I flew just above the treetops and as we passed by his home, you could hear a shout from the back of the cabin, "Jimmy's home!"

One time, I flew Jimmy into Palm Beach International, but he did not have a ride home. I offered him a ride in my Z sports car. It was a funny scene, because it seemed like a setup, but it wasn't. When we got in the car and I turned the key, the cassette tape player started playing Jimmy's music. I had told him that I listened to his music often, so he already knew I was a big fan. One time, he allowed Kelley and me to have a photo taken with him standing in front of the Learjet. He even went to the trouble to autograph it for us. I still have the picture of the three of us standing on the ramp, with the entrance door to the jet open and our arms around one another. I am on the left with a broad grin, a Clark Gable mustache, and a sharp captain's uniform. Kelley is standing between us, wearing aviator sunglasses, sporting windswept hair, and a smiling broad grin on her face. Jimmy stands grinning with a zebra print shirt, baseball hat, and sunglasses. The autograph says, "To Joe and Kelley, best wishes, Jimmy Buffett, thanks for the great flight!"

Later on in my career, after I became a captain with Piedmont Airlines based in Miami, we had several flights in and out of Key West. At the time we had a very funny flight attendant, Cindy Joyce, who would always close the cockpit door with a joke, like a line from the comedy movie, *Airplane*. I would say, "Surely it's not time to close the door." She would reply back smiling, "Yes, it is time to close the door, and don't call me Shirley." She would say it with the same deadpan delivery that Leslie Nielsen used to use. It was pretty hilarious.

On one occasion, Cindy came up to the cockpit and told me that she had a special passenger in first class. I thought it was another one of her jokes, so I asked her who it was. She told me it was Jimmy Buffett. I said, "Cool! Ask him to come up here." She said, "No, I can't do that. He is a passenger in first class; it's just not done." I then explained to Cindy that I actually knew Jimmy, and said, "Tell Jimmy that Joe Townsend is the captain, and he would like to say hello." When Jimmy entered the cockpit in a tropical shirt and shorts, he was grinning from ear to ear. It was great to see him again. I asked him if he would like to ride in the jump seat and he accepted my offer. Of course, this was very much against the rules to have a civilian sitting in the cockpit with the pilots, but he did and I let him. It's too late to get a violation now, so for the first time, I am able to share the story publicly.

One of the things I love about my entire career in flying was that I got to meet lots of great people. I met Jimmy Buffet and someone else in my life named Bob Benz. You have heard of Jimmy because he is a celebrity. You probably haven't heard of Bob. Bob is a great guy and we shared a passion for life, but even more for flying.

In the winter of 1991, Kelley and I went on a ski trip to Breckenridge, Colorado. We met our friends there, Bobby and BJ, who introduced us to another set of friends, a couple named Bob and Lisa Bentz. We got along well on this trip, and I enjoyed talking to them. Bob and I both were good skiers, and we skied together on the blue and black trails while the other, slower skiers stuck to the green and the blue courses. Wimps! Bob and I also shared a passion for planes and a love of flying. He was an ophthalmologist, and he had his private pilot's license, but had not flown since before medical school. After meeting me, his fire for flying was reignited, and he wanted to get back into flying again. I had a flight instructor certificate, so I was happy to help him back into his addiction to flying. Ironically, he rented airplanes from the same flying club that used to lease my first plane from me.

Bob rented several different airplanes that we flew together. I was helping him learn some of the more subtle aspects of flying and helping him get his instrument training. In August of 1994, we rented a Mooney 201 and flew on an instrument flight plan to Key West and back. Unfortunately, due to circumstances beyond our control, we never actually got to do the back part of our flight plan.

I was looking forward to flying to Key West with Bob, as he was a pleasant fellow and we got along well. The flight went flawlessly, and at about 4,000 feet we could see the runway as we started descending. The sun was out. The sky was clear and the weather was perfect. We were in our descent when the engine suddenly went quiet. I am, and have always been, a calm pilot. Calm pilots think more clearly and are able to make better decisions. Once I realized the engine was quiet, I immediately took over the controls to slow the plane down to the best possible gliding speed. I then scrambled all over the cockpit, changing the fuel selector to the other fuel tank, changing the mixture to full rich, and trying to get the propeller to full forward. I had no luck. Bob took over the radio as we were on an instrument flight plan. I had him tell the control tower in Key West that we were officially declaring an emergency.

It's amazing how quickly the control tower answers when you say you have an emergency. The approach controller asked, "What is the nature of your emergency?" Bob turned to me and asked me what to say back to the controller. I replied, "Bob, how about ENGINE FAILURE!!" They got the message pretty clearly. There was a runway at Navy Key West Air Station that was perfectly in line with our flight path. Bob told them that we wished to land there. The controller replied in his controller voice: "Roger, Mooney. You are cleared to land any runway."

Even though I kept the gear up to prevent more drag as we were gliding, we still did not have enough altitude to make it to the runway, and there was a huge obstacle in between us. The unpleasant obstacle between us was a nasty set of high-tension power lines that could have easily ruined our day. That was the bad news. The good news was that the water was calm and not too choppy. So I decided that the best recourse was to ditch the plane just short of the shoreline and, hopefully, before the power lines. My friend, Bob, was very concerned about the high-tension power lines. He said, "Hey, Joe, those power lines are looking mighty close!" I was concentrating and replied to him with a very clipped, "OK." I was still trying to get that engine started up again.

A minute later, as we got closer, Bob said frantically, "Hey, Joe, those lines are looking close." I acknowledged Bob in a distracted way, because I was still doing everything in my power to try to get the engine restarted. I made sure the fuel pump was on, that the mixture was full rich; I switched fuel tanks and turned the magneto switch. Beads of sweat were popping up on my forehead. The power lines were still looking us in the face, and we were now only a few hundred feet from shore. We were moving fast, but it all seemed like a movie playing in slow motion.

At this point, Bob became outright frantic about the power lines and said, "Hey, Joe! Those power lines are in our way!" I did not even look over at him; I needed to keep my eyes on the landing, but I said reassuringly, "Will you relax. We are not going to make it that far. Let's radio Navy Key West approach and tell them that we are going to be in the water real soon." Bob nervously radioed the approach tower. His hand was shaking with anticipation of us hitting the water soon. As we neared the water, the wind was very light. All of the conditions were perfect that day, and I made one of the smoothest ditchings possible.

We slowly glided onto the water. Once the plane came to a stop, we opened the doors and stepped out onto the low wing. We stood on the wing in an area where the water depth was only about 4 feet. It wasn't too long (I guess news travels fast when a plane ditches in the ocean) before some very nice divers came to our rescue, picking us up in their Boston Whaler boat. That was really nice of them to help us out, and it gave them a story to tell their families that evening. The approach controller dispatched a Florida Marine patrol helicopter to pick us up at the shoreline and take us over to Key West International Airport. We both called our wives and told them we were going to be a little late coming home. Next, I called the Chandelle flying club to let them know that their Mooney plane did not float very well.

We sat down and talked through the whole incident with the FAA controller and flight service station. They realized both of us were not at fault and that there was nothing we could have done to prevent the ditch landing, and they wrote their reports to reflect that.

Bob and I were kind of tired of flying at that point. So we rented a car and drove back to West Palm Beach. During our little adventure, we worked up quite an appetite. As we passed through Key Largo, we stopped at my favorite restaurant there called *The Fish House* for some yummy and totally delectable Jamaican jerk-style catch of the day. It's amazing the crazy stuff a pilot will do for a good meal.

After the plane was pulled out of the water, it was thoroughly inspected by the National Transportation Safety Board. The first thing they looked for was fuel quantity, and they found that the tanks were more than half full. Then, after checking through the engine, they found that the tower shaft, which was connected to the magnetos, was sheared. I know that you're probably saying to yourself, "What the heck is a magneto?" Well, it's like the type of distributor that used to be on a car before electronic ignition was available. There are always two on an engine, so that in the case that one fails, the other can take over. However, there's only one tower shaft, and if the tower shaft fails, you just got shafted. Bob and I really got shafted. We were fortunate to land safely (I should say ditch safely), so we celebrated with a good meal to comfort our empty bellies and dry off our wet feet. Life really is good.

Joe and I had finished our sandwiches long before he finished his story. We sat in this café for several hours as he talked and I listened. Dozens of people must have passed by us, but I didn't notice one of them. Joe spoke enthusiastically about his flight career, and for the first time I caught a real glimpse into the adrenaline life of a pilot. I hung onto every word of his story about ditching his plane in Key West and felt the adrenaline pump through me just as if I was there. Joe has faced death multiple times and survived to tell the stories! And I couldn't believe that his life afforded him opportunities to cross paths with such successful celebrities like Jimmy Buffett. Joe has truly lived a tremendous life. As he finished up his story, I glanced down at my watch and realized that it was getting close to his flight time.

"Well, Joe, I should probably get you back to the airport."

"Sounds good. Boy, I think I like Philly cheese steaks."

"Great," I said. "I'm glad you enjoyed it."

"I guess we should go. I got a flight to catch."

"Let's go, Mr. Joe."

Endnote

1. The Rolling Stones, "You Can't Always Get What You Want," *Let It Bleed* (1969).

Chapter 6

Clinging to Lifelines

Pain nourishes courage. You can't be brave if you've only had wonderful things happen to you.—Mary Tyler Moore[1]

It had been several weeks since Joe had flown in for lunch and I had heard the latest installment of his story. Each time we talked, I took copious notes to help compile his book. There was something about Joe's life that continued to captivate and inspire me. He had faced adversity many times, but something within him caused him to rise up. I was drawn to it and longed to put my finger on what it was exactly that made Joe such an overcomer. Between conversations, I couldn't wait to hear about the next aspect of his life.

One sunny Saturday morning, I picked up the phone and called Joe. "Hello, Joseppy. How are you?" I greeted Joe enthusiastically.

"Oh, hello there, buddy! Doing *fantastic!* What's going on?" he replied, equally happy to talk.

"I am busy as a bee, Joe, but as you know that's a good thing," I admitted.

"Well, I sure enjoyed our visit in Philadelphia a few weeks ago. That Philly cheese steak was everything I expected and more," Joe said kindly.

"Yep, those were pretty good. Next time you come to Philly I would be happy to buy you another one. Or I could just send you one in the mail," I said chuckling.

Joe laughed back, "Somehow, I don't think it would be too fresh by the time it got to Colorado!"

"Yeah, that's true. Well, Mr. Joe, I really would love to know what happened to you after the crash, if you don't find it too upsetting to tell me," I prompted.

"No. I don't mind," he said. "It is a story that needs to be told, and I want you to know exactly what happened. I mean you are the one who's going to help me write a book about it."

The plane was traveling at close to 70 miles an hour when it crashed. My lovely wife, Kelley, and my beautiful daughter Laura were both killed instantly in the crash; they died from traumatic head injuries. The human body that God has created is a magnificent machine. Sometimes it's amazing what we can all survive. But there are times when the awesome velocity of speed and impact is just too much. For Kelley and Laura, that was the case. I tell you, all of those rescuers and paramedics worked really hard that day to try to save us all. It must have been heart wrenching for them to discover that they couldn't; in some ways, the rescue efforts had failed. But it was not their fault. I've always been thankful for their efforts in that they tried so hard with everything they had.

After I was extracted from the wreckage of the plane, Tara and I were taken to Dorminy Medical Center in Fitzgerald, Georgia. After doing triage and reviewing how incredibly critical our injuries were, they treated us briefly, and then whisked us off in separate ambulances to Phoebe Putney Memorial Hospital in Albany, Georgia, which was a renowned head-trauma center.

I, Joe Townsend, am a man. As a man, I am also a human being. Each of us as human beings has a soul. But keep in mind that physically we are also a brilliantly designed collection of organs, muscles, tendons, bones, and nerves. My injuries were so extensive that sometimes it still amazes me that I survived at all.

As we descended, the plane dropped steeply as a result of the wing stalling. We had just cleared the approach light tower. When the plane hit the ground, my forehead slammed into the instrument panel and the artificial horizon knob hit me so hard it broke through my skull. I'm sure that you have hit your head at some point in your lifetime. Maybe you were getting out of a car and banged it on a doorframe. Maybe you got a hard helmet-to-helmet hit in football. But nothing, and I mean nothing, could compare to the brute force with which that knob slammed into my forehead. Due to my severe head impact, it caused a contrecoup injury, which blinded me temporarily. I thank God for that because it prevented me from seeing the wreckage and my mortally wounded family around me.

I found a simplified explanation of what a contrecoup brain injury actually is on Wikipedia to help you understand what happened to me.

> In head injury, a coup injury occurs under the site of impact with an object, and a contrecoup injury occurs on the side opposite the area that was impacted. Coup and contrecoup injury is associated with cerebral contusion, a type of traumatic brain injury in which the brain is bruised. Coup and contrecoup injuries can occur individually or together. When a moving object impacts the stationary head, coup injuries are typical, while contrecoup injuries are produced

when the moving head strikes a stationary object.

In a coup injury, the head stops abruptly and the brain collides with the inside of the skull.

Coup and contrecoup injuries are considered focal brain injuries, those that occur in a particular spot in the brain, as opposed to diffuse injuries, which occur over a more widespread area.

The mechanism for the injuries, especially contrecoup injuries, is a subject of much debate. It is likely that inertia is involved in the injuries, e.g. when the brain keeps moving after the skull is stopped by a fixed object or when the brain remains still after the skull is accelerated by an impact with a moving object. Alternately, movement of cerebrospinal fluid following a trauma may play a role in the injury.[2]

My brain damage was in my occipital lobe, which is like the hard drive for your eyesight, and in my cerebellum, which controlled all of my motor skills and balance. After the crash my cerebellum and occipital lobe were all gonzo—shaken and scrambled. I was totally blind and had no motor skills.

Neurosurgeon Dr. Robert Hanchey worked on Tara while I was being worked on by other surgeons. After an hour of working on her furiously, they could not save her. She too died of severe head trauma, and my littlest angel flew off to be with her mommy and big sister in Heaven.

I was not there, because I was in another room being operated on. But I often wonder how it was for Dr. Hanchey. Was he sad, or was he able to maintain a surgeon's dispassionate mindset? Did he cry? Was it harder for him because Tara was a little one? I wonder. Those are the days when being a neurosurgeon must be a tough road to hoe; it must be painful to see the loss. I appreciate him trying to save my little darling one, and I know that he did his best. That is all I would ever ask. I hope that he was at peace and did not agonize over it. After Tara was gone, I was told that Dr. Hanchey told his team that it is now time to go to work on her daddy.

After that, Dr. Hanchey joined the other surgeons to work on me. He was a very skilled neurosurgeon and placed a titanium mesh over the hole in my forehead. The great and steady artistic hands of a plastic surgeon sewed up the large opening and there is no scar. But if you put your hand to my forehead today you can clearly feel where the hole is. You know, when I was younger and a little crazier, adults would ask me, "Joe, what is wrong with you? Do you have a hole in your head or something?" Now if someone asked me that question, I can say, "Why, yes I do. Would you like to feel it?" I'm sure that would get an interesting response.

The second worst injury I received was almost as horrific. My legs and feet were damaged when the plane hit the ground. I suffered compound fractures in the joints of both of my feet. When a body is traveling at a high rate of speed, any sudden, high-force stop (such as the plane crashing into the ground) can cause this type of injury. In fact, this is fairly common. While the results are predictable and common, the damage that it creates is devastating. My body stopped moving due to impact with the ground, but my joints and bones were still in a forward motion. This sudden stop created strain and massive tension on my skin, muscles, tendons, and bones. When my skin failed, my anklebones also failed and fractured, and as a result they were exposed to the outside world. In more simple terms, both of my feet were nearly torn off at the ankle joints. This is a devastating injury that continues to plague me.

In addition to my mangled feet, my legs were bent backward at the knees. I suffered compound fractures of both knees as well as a compound fracture of my left femur. Orthopedic surgeons are the gifted structural mechanics of the medical world. Doctors used steel rods, plates, and screws to put me back together again. I am a modern version of Humpty Dumpty. Because of my internal injuries, I also had to have part of my small intestine removed in surgery.

As you can imagine, when my feet were nearly torn from my body, there was an amazing and enormous amount of blood loss. I lost so much blood that they transfused 15 pints of blood into me over the course of the next 12 hours. Medicine is a riddle; there's a balance between the treatment that heals and the effect of the treatment. All the new transfused blood in my system saved me. Ironically, that same new blood also nearly killed me. In fact, it did kill me. All of the new blood gathered around my heart and formed a blood clot in my heart so that it stopped beating for 45 minutes. The resuscitation team at the hospital worked on me until they were able to bring me back to life. I also suffered a stroke, and my immediate prognosis was extremely grim. The doctor came out to talk to Kelley's cousins and said that it was unlikely that I would live through that night. My injuries were so severe that no one on the medical staff at the hospital really believed that I would survive. Somehow, deep within me, I believed within my soul that I was going to make it. I somehow just knew.

Back in Florida, my father was pacing back and forth while my mother, sisters, and brother were praying. My father and sister Mary Anne were on the first flight the next morning to Tallahassee where they rented a car to drive over to Albany.

For the next ten days, friends and relatives visited and looked in on me. I was not able to talk to them and respond, as I had lapsed into a deep coma. I was entirely dependent on a ventilator to breathe; I was not breathing at all on my own. A patient can only stay on the ventilator with an endotracheal tube (which goes down the mouth into the throat) for a certain number of days before the tube starts to damage the tissue in the throat.

The doctors conferred and decided that they needed to give me a tracheostomy, a routine procedure to surgically open an airway by cutting a hole in the throat. This would have meant having a permanent opening into my trachea through my neck that would allow air to flow to my lungs. Generally speaking, the medical community understands that people who have this procedure done are finished with living. They were predicting that I would be confined to a bed and hooked up to a ventilator for the rest of my life.

WOW! Even when I think about it today, this thought is reprehensible and horrifying. That grim quality of life would have been unbearable, not only for me but for my family. I am blessed, however, to have my sister Mary Ann, who is incredibly smart and understands medicine because she is a trained registered nurse. She is a fighter, a little medical pit bull. She put her foot down and said that she would not allow the doctor to perform this procedure on me under any circumstance. My sister thought that I was responsive and could eventually be weaned from the ventilator.

She argued with the doctors, who disagreed with her. The doctors were pessimistic and thought that I had very little chance for recovery with any quality of life. She knew that I was going to make it, and she said through tears with a shaky voice," I am not going to let you do this. We're not carting off my brother Joe to a nursing home to die." The whole family in Florida was in despair and shock. My sister continued to fight at my bed-side. She begged and cajoled the nurses not to sedate me, because it would help me lighten up neurologically, so that I could come out of the coma. They were under doctors' orders.

Although I was in a coma, my sister saw me respond to certain voices. One of the voices belonged to a woman named Angie Harrell who would come to the hospital each day to visit her father who was in the ICU. She would also come into my room every day and talk to me even though I was in a coma. My sister noticed that I responded each time Angie was around, and that truly convinced my sister that I was still "in there." The nurses were following orders, which included heavy sedation. My sister stayed around the clock to keep them from sedating me. Finally, on December 10, I was extubated and breathing on my own.

It is amazing when you think about how certain things happen in your life. What if I did not have Mary Ann as my nurse expert and advocate? What if Angie did not have a father who was in ICU? She would have never known that I was there. Why did I respond to Angie's voice?

Was her voice similar to Kelley's? Is that why I responded to her? I will never know. I don't have the wisdom and the understanding to know such things. Only God knows.

While I was floating in a comatose state in a hospital room in Georgia, the funeral for Kelly, Laura, and Tara was being held in West Palm Beach. By the time I regained consciousness, my dear three angels had already been buried in a plot of dirt at the Queen of Peace cemetery on the western edge of town. Due to the severe head trauma, I thought that I was alone in the airplane and did not even know that they had died. I do vaguely remember wondering why they weren't visiting me in the hospital. I came out of my coma and cleared the cobwebs out of my mind. A night nurse came into my room, and I asked her where my wife and kids were. She came over to my bedside, looked down at me, and said in a soft tone, "Why, Joe, all three of your girls are now angels up in Heaven." I knew in my heart that it could not possibly be true. I slowly explained to the nurse that I was the only one in the plane, and that she did not know what she was talking about. I knew that my father and my sister would be back to see me the following morning to set the record straight. I planned on reporting this nurse for saying things that weren't true and getting me upset.

The next morning, Mary Anne and my Dad came to visit me as usual. I was very irritated and shared my terrible encounter with the nurse the night before. With tears in her eyes, my sister grabbed my hand and told me that the nurse had told me the truth. I can't say that I cried because crying doesn't do justice to describe my level of grief. I sobbed. I sobbed so hard that there was an actual pain in my heart. The air in me was expelled, and I felt like a sharp dagger was rotating and tearing my heart right out of my chest. I yelled and thrashed around in my bed.

People often say, "There are no good words to describe it," when trying to articulate something unfathomable. I now know exactly what that means. There have been many, many times over the years since that horrible moment that I have tried to describe what it feels like to lose your entire world. I'm a simple man, and I'm at a loss for words. It is just not possible to describe that level of absolute and completely crushing devastation. My entire life had always revolved around two things: my family and my flying. Now, with the blink of an eye, the snap of a finger, and the silent, gentle sweep of a second hand on a watch, I had lost everything. At that moment, while I was sitting in that hospital bed in Georgia, I could not imagine a life without my beautiful wife and my daughters. How could they possibly be gone?

I went to sleep, woke up, and they had vanished from my life. How would I face getting out of bed in the morning, expecting the giggles and laughter, the pitter-patter of little feet running to jump into my arms, only to be greeted by stone-cold silence? How could it be that when I walked in the door of my home that my wife Kelley would not be there to hug me? How? The blackboard of my life had been completely erased, washed, as if my old life never existed. At that moment, I was a helpless, hopeless empty shell of a man.

Somehow, someway, I knew in the tiniest recesses of my being, in the architecture of my singular cells, I wanted to go on. I just had to figure out a way to do it alone. I did have the unending support, strength, resolve, and comfort of my great family and their many friends who were loyal and too numerous to mention. But at the end of the day, I would lie in my hospital bed in the dark and realize that for the first time in many, many years I was truly and totally alone.

Thus began the most difficult and trying journey of my whole life. It was the journey to reclaim a life that had been shattered into one million pieces. It was trying to figure out how to put those pieces together again and still survive.

While I lay in that hospital in Georgia, my dear friend Danny (who fell off his bike at 13 when we were on my paper route) had been working to get an air-ambulance flight to bring me back to West Palm Beach. I was moved to West Palm 17 days after my crash. I always wanted to go home, to be surrounded in the hospital by my friends and family and the doctors that I knew. I was discharged from the hospital in Georgia on December 17, 1996. I was taken to the Albany Airport by ambulance and a Cessna Citation twin-engine jet was waiting for me. When I saw the plane, I remembered flying air-ambulance trips myself on the same twin-engine jet or on Learjets. My devoted sister Mary Ann flew with us, while my father returned the rental car to Tallahassee and flew a commercial airline home.

I will never forget that flight. Ever! Oh, that horrible, horrible flight. For reasons that I will never be able to understand, they had me on a hard board on top of a stretcher. My back did not hurt until then. Imagine being battered and bruised while lying on a simple piece of plywood for a couple of hours. It was the worst ride of my entire life. My younger sister Elizabeth met us at the West Palm Beach airport for the ambulance ride to St. Mary's. We were also greeted by my sister Rosie, Bob Benz, and my good buddy Joey Piazza, who was a copilot for me at BizJet. I have to tell you, it was very uplifting and humbling to see how many people were there to meet me.

When I arrived at St. Mary's hospital, Kelley's OB/GYN Dr. Jay Trabin admitted me. Dr. Frank Cook, my neighbor, friend, and orthopedic surgeon, was also waiting for me. The ladies would describe him as tall, dark, and handsome. He was in his late 30s, incredibly fit, and had a wonderfully friendly bedside manner. He liked Jimmy Buffett music so much that he played it in the operating room when he did my reconstructive surgeries. He was easygoing and a very likable fellow. He was also a great doctor. He escorted me to the X-ray room so he could review my injuries right away.

He knew that it was possible I had developed an infection in my feet, so they had me in a hyperbaric chamber every day to increase my healing. The chamber sends oxygen throughout the entire body so that it reaches the places where it is difficult for antibiotics to get to. I'm so grateful to Dr. Cook, as I believe that this treatment is what saved my feet from gangrene and amputation. Oh sure, I could have been fitted with prosthetics, but

I am very glad to have my own feet, even though they don't always work like they used to. Prosthetics can never replace the natural equipment that God gave you!

My sisters took turns every night sleeping on an air mattress beside my bed. They were there to comfort and help me but mainly to just be by my side. Due to the brain injury, I could only see shadows at that time. I also could not walk or feed myself. I was in critical, but stable, condition. After surviving the crash and undergoing multiple surgeries, it was a gift to have my loving family surround me with support. I will be forever grateful to them. My amazing sister Rose was 8½ months pregnant with her first child, and she still came to the hospital and lay on the air mattress when it was her turn. Bless her heart.

I was so blessed to have so many visitors. There were almost always friends and family in my room, and it was often standing room only. Many airline friends even flew in from out of town, including a few classmates from my new-hire class at Piedmont Airlines. I remember my friend James Ray flew in from Charlotte to see me. I was in physical therapy and he walked around the hospital hallways with me. Along with Laurette, my physical therapist, he held onto my gait belt and helped me through therapy. On the weekends, many different friends came and pushed me outside in my wheelchair to get some fresh air. My friend, Dr. Rusty Oenbrink, liked to get his power walk in by rolling me around the hospital grounds. It's true that you never really know how many friends you have. I always had a feeling that I had many friends, but the number of friends who called, wrote, visited, and did things for me was way beyond my comprehension. I can never thank any of them enough in a thousand lifetimes.

Every day, I spent an hour in the hyperbaric chamber to get oxygen to my feet to heal them. To get to the chamber, I had to be lifted onto a stretcher, with all my hoses still connected, and then wheeled down to the chamber room. The chamber was a long steel tube with a clear Plexiglas window on top that I slid into. They would seal the door, pressurize the tube, and send in lots of healthy oxygen. I could watch movies through the

Plexiglas window on top. It was working well, and I felt like I was making progress. Unfortunately, I had to stop after a few weeks when I got fluid in my lungs.

Oh swell! Happy New Year to me! It certainly was not what I was hoping for. This also meant that someone was going to have to drain the fluid out of my lungs. So the hospital called up central casting, and found the perfect actor for the role. His name was Dr. Sadist. Of course that was not his real name, but if Hollywood were ever casting a movie about a World War II concentration camp, this man would play the lead torturer. It sometimes seems to me that some people in the medical community don't just dislike empathy, but *enjoy* inflicting pain on another human being.

This doctor took a big, thick, sharp-ended tube and jammed it in between my ribs. This was all done with absolutely no anesthetic. I have a very high pain tolerance, but I was screaming bloody murder from the pain, and I'm sure other patients on the floor wondered what was going on in my room. He just kept pushing that tube deeper and deeper and deeper into my lung; it felt like it was being pushed all the way to the other side of my chest. When he was done, I was pale, sweaty, and exhausted. After several days, the fluid drained out and the tube came out very easily with no pain. Thank God!

In the middle of January, I reached a milestone in my recovery, and I was moved to the rehabilitation floor. That was a big deal, because I thought that I was finally making progress. When you're really sick and weak, each development (like being moved to another floor) really boosts your morale. They gave me a room with an extra bed for my sisters and friends to sleep in. That was real nice for both of us, because I had friends and family close by and they were no longer sleeping on an uncomfortable air mattress. In late January, I told everyone that I was grateful for their support, but didn't need them to stay through the night anymore. The nurses' station was conveniently right outside my door.

The entire time I had been in the hospital I had an IV stuck into my arm. Needless to say, having an IV in your arm is very hard on your veins. My arms were black and blue, and the IV had to be changed on occasion when a vein was no longer cooperating. The medical team decided that it would be best for me to have a central IV in my chest. I too thought that was a great idea, as it would give me a little more freedom of movement. I did not know, however, what the procedure involved. They needed to insert a two-inch, sharp piece of stainless steel into my chest. So who did the hospital decide would be best suited for this remarkably unpleasant task? If you guessed Dr. Sadist, you win the grand prize. That's right, Dr. Sadist made his triumphant return.

I started sweating and shaking as soon as he entered my room. Again, he decided it would not be a good idea to use anesthesia (local or otherwise), and he lowered the head of my bed so that my feet were about a foot higher than my head. This gave him the right angle to aggressively push the hunk of pointed metal into my chest, and I screamed bloody murder as he stabbed me. A central IV was used to administer drugs directly into the bloodstream. At that point, I was ready for some morphine. I actually did not like taking drugs, so I had them wean me off of the narcotics fairly quickly. I could have legitimately and easily stayed on the drug plan, but I thought that it would slow me down, and I wanted to be up and at 'em as soon as I could.

My physical therapist, Laurette, was a sweet woman who hailed from South Africa. She was patient and always had a bright, friendly smile. She was probably about 30 years old, had brown hair, and stood about 5 feet 5 inches. She had smooth, clear, tan skin. She had a lilting accent that sounded slightly British to me. She always had a happy and positive disposition. She was not the drill sergeant type, nor was she bossy. She instinctively knew that the way to motivate me was to encourage me with kind words and a smile.

Initially, we focused the physical therapy on restoring movement to my lower extremities. Later on, we worked on getting me out of bed and into a wheelchair. After that, I worked on getting up and walking between parallel bars that offered support and balance. Toward the end of therapy, as I was getting close to being discharged, I was walking using a gait belt. The gait belt is a wide belt that is wrapped tightly around your waist. The therapist helps hold you up and steadies you as you relearn to walk.

I also had occupational therapy, which consisted of hand-and-eye coordination exercises like tossing a big, brightly colored beach ball back and forth. We also worked on fine motor skills, like stacking brightly colored cups and threading nuts onto bolts. I had never seen a captain on an airline stack cups in the cockpit, but I understood that the purpose of these exercises was to regain my motor skills.

I also needed speech therapy because I had experienced a stroke. I learned to make different sounds and exercised my speech with different words and songs. I wish I could remember my therapist's name, but I can't. She asked me what song I would like to work on in order to improve my speaking abilities. It probably comes as no surprise to you that my choice was *Cheeseburger in Paradise* by Jimmy Buffett. Come to think of it, for a song with word choices, I picked a doozy of a song for speech rehab.

> Tried to amend my carnivorous habits,
> Made it nearly seventy days,
> Losin' weight without speed, eatin' sunflower seeds,
> Drinkin' lots of carrot juice and soakin' up rays.
>
> But at night I'd had these wonderful dreams
> Some kind of sensuous treat
> Not zucchini, fettuccine or bulgur wheat
> But a big warm bun and a huge hunk of meat.
>
> Cheeseburger in Paradise,
> Heaven on earth with an onion slice,
> Not too particular not too precise
> I'm just a cheeseburger in Paradise.[3]

The Parrot Head Club (the Jimmy Buffett fan club) heard that I was in the hospital and knew that I used to fly Jimmy around as a pilot. The president of the club came to visit me in early February. They told me that they wanted to hold a benefit to honor my girls. They wanted to use the proceeds to purchase a gazebo to go on the playground at Laura's Pre-K school. The benefit was on a Saturday night, and someone picked me up so I was able to attend. At that point, I was still wheelchair-bound and learning how to transfer to a car took some getting used to.

The benefit was a great turnout of all my family and friends and hundreds of Buffett fans. They raised enough money for a large gazebo. I sure wish I could remember the president's name, as I appreciated how kind he was, but I have an excuse—an airplane hit me in the head! He came in to visit me the next week to tell me about the successful benefit results. He asked me if there was anything he could do for me. I knew that Jimmy Buffett was planning a concert at the Choral Sky Amphitheater the following Saturday. So I asked, "How about backstage passes to Jimmy's concert?" He said it was a huge undertaking, but that he would do his best. Great guy that he was, he came back in a couple days and said, "It's a go!"

On the day of Jimmy's concert, my sister Rose and her husband Shawn were having a baptismal for their new son Eamonn. They asked if I would be his godfather. I was deeply honored and said yes. Shawn picked me up from the hospital and loaded me and my wheels into the car. We went to the baptismal, had some dinner at my sister Mary Anne's home, and then Shawn and I went to the concert. Shawn and I used the two backstage passes and entered the reception area for the VIPs, which included food and Corona beers. I wasn't into the beer, but it sure was nice to have a change from the hospital food I had been eating for weeks.

My friend Randy Leslie was working as Jimmy's pilot at the time. We saw him lounging in the VIP area, and he sent word to Jimmy that I was there. A huge mountain of a security guard escorted Shawn and I to the area where the artists were. Shawn was pushing me in my wheelchair. When Jimmy saw me, he came over and bent down and gave me a big hug.

He said he had intended to come and visit me in the hospital, and he was glad that I was there as I had saved him the trip.

On my birthday, March 16, my sister Rose came to visit me in the evening. I was wondering why none of my family or friends had stopped by to sing me Happy Birthday. I mean I never expected it, but it still is always nice when it happens. I guess in my beat-up state, I was also still a little too sensitive, which was understandable. Rose said she wanted to visit a family friend, Patty Lewis, who had just delivered a baby in the hospital birthing center. She rolled me down the hall in my wheelchair, but instead of heading toward the birthing center, she wheeled me into the cafeteria to get a bowl of ice cream. It was about 7 PM, and I told her that I thought it was closed. She completely ignored what I said and just kept pushing me faster and faster. We rolled into the cafeteria, and to my delight and amazement, there were close to 100 family members and friends, shouting, smiling, and singing a raucous round of "Happy Birthday to Joe." This was an awesome surprise, and my eyes filled up with tears as I realized how blessed I was to have the love of family and friends. That was the one and only surprise birthday party I have ever had in my life. It was the sweetest and the best gift ever.

By mid-March, my hospital stay was coming to an end. I vividly remember walking between the parallel bars without holding on for about 5 on St. Patrick's Day. This was a monumental achievement. Five feet does not seem like much, but for me it might as well have been a mile. I was feeling really great, as I knew I was well on my road to recovery. My dad came to pick me up when I was discharged on March 18. He loaded up my wheelchair and we were out of there.

After being cared for and being in a hospital for so long, I was delighted to finally have my freedom. I was very nervous, however, about going to the home where Kelley, the girls, and I had been so happy. On the way home, we stopped by Bob Bentz's office to test my vision, and on that day it measured 20/300. That was a lot better than being totally blind, but my vision still had a ways to go. My sister Rose was waiting for me at home with her husband Shawn and baby Eamonn. They were going to live with me and help nurse me back to better health. I still needed full-time care.

I entered a new phase of my life, feeling the joy of regaining my health, the freedom of being out of the hospital, and the despair of not knowing how I was going to live my life again alone. For the first time in my life, there was no road map or aeronautical chart to guide me.

I was amazed at the sheer enormity of the recovery and the loss, pain, and more pain this man had had to endure. For months. Yet he was steadfast like a rock. People struggle to overcome injuries or to recover from surgery, but Joe had the triple play; recovery from grief, physical injury and recovery, and loss of ability to make a living as a pilot—all at once. Joe is like an amazing watch that had been run over by a bulldozer, but just kept on ticking. I was wondering what made him able to keep ticking, to keep going despite all of his adversity.

Reflecting on his story, I think it was, first, his iron will and never-give-up attitude; second, he was blessed with an amazing support system of friends; and third, his faith gave him strength and comfort in knowing he would see the girls again one day. I felt like, if Joe could overcome all that, then anyone else should be able to overcome anything. There is hope in knowing it can be done and who those that face tremendous adversity can survive and thrive and eventually lead a happy life.

"Well, Joe," I said, "I have heard of tough guys before, but you are a real tough guy. You just don't give up!"

"Nope!" Joe agreed.

"Sounds like you are really blessed with all the friends you have," I said admiringly.

"There is no doubt about that," he replied.

"Joe, I appreciate your time today. I gotta run to log onto a conference call," I said, wrapping up our conversation.

"OK buddy, see ya."

"Have a great day, Joe," I said as I hung up the phone.

ENDNOTES

1. Mary Tyler Moore, quoted on *Joy of Quotes;* http://www.joyofquotes.com/courage_quotes.html; accessed March 29, 2011.

2. "Coup Contrecoup Injury," *Wikipedia;* http://en.wikipedia.org/wiki/Coup_contrecoup_injury; accessed May 19, 2011.

3. Buffet, Jimmy, "Cheeseburger in Paradise," *Son of a Son of a Sailor* (1978).

Chapter 7

Home Is Where the Heart Is

Part of every misery is, so to speak, the misery's shadow or reflection: the fact that you don't merely suffer but have to keep on thinking about the fact that you suffer. I not only live each endless day in grief, but live each day thinking about living each day in grief.—C.S. Lewis[1]

I was sitting at my computer reading an e-mail from Joe.

"Hey, Shawn, when do you want to catch up?" he wrote.

I wrote back, "Let's talk on Friday."

On Friday, I called Joe and he answered in his usual chipper tone.

"Hello, Shawn!"

"Hey, Joe," I said. "You sound a little out of breath. You OK?"

"Well," he said chuckling, "I just stumbled over our big hound doggy on the way to the phone."

"Oh, wow. Are you sure you're OK?" I questioned.

"Yep. I am doing fabulous," he replied.

"So last time we talked about the story, you were getting out of the hospital—right? So then what happened?"

"Well, I had many more challenges to face than I expected…"

So it was finally time to go home after being in the hospital for so very long, and I was glad to be going home. As Dorothy said in *The Wizard of Oz,* "There is no place like home." It is true. It's an odd experience when you pull up in front of your own house and everything looks so new and different. Odd.

Little did I know it, but I was in for the shock of my life as I was rolled up in a wheelchair to the door of my home. Maybe it's not the biggest shock of my life, but it certainly was one of the top three and definitely one of the most insulting. When I got inside of my home, I discovered that Kelley's family had entered the house while I was in the hospital. They emptied out the girls' playroom and removed all of their clothes, shoes, and pretty much anything that they could think of. I could not even believe my own eyes. I sat blinking. It was all…gone! I felt so violated when they came into *my* home and took things that they did not even ask about. I was grieving greatly and could not believe that they had done this. I was crushed. This felt like the ultimate act of betrayal.

I called them later that day to ask them about it, and they told me they had sold the girls' clothes at a consignment store for around $550. They told me they would happily return the money and anything else they had taken that I still wanted. I was in a rage. The irony was that legally everything was mine. They were all in my home and not their own. In the will, of course, everything of Kelley's was mine to do with as I saw fit—totally mine.

A few months later, they had the audacity to come again for more things, like a piano Kelley had grown up with in her parents' home. I discovered later that they took Kelley's camera and several of her Louis Vuitton and Gucci purses. They left behind a few things like a plastic slide belonging to the girls and, most importantly, Laura's little art desk. I had great memories of my little girl sitting at that desk coloring. She always sat there when she was drawing her pictures. That little desk still sits in my home today.

I tried to be as understanding as I could about Kelley's family. I realized that they were grieving and had tons of heartache for the loss of Kelley, Laura, and Tara. Even though I could have legally done so, I did not press the issue, because, after all, these were not things I would use myself, so I needed to let it go. It didn't make it any easier. Believe it or not, Kelley's mom even asked my sisters, "Why is it that Joe survived and not the girls?" I understand that she was hurt and probably bitter. It's hard not to be when you've experienced such a great loss. It was a devastating loss for all of us.

What really hurt me was that they didn't seem to recognize or acknowledge that I had done my best to get that severely crippled airplane on the ground safely. The last thing I ever would have wanted in my life was to lose my precious family. But I had certainly paid, and paid dearly, for what happened that day in Georgia.

The next step for me to regain my life was to continue physical therapy at home. I was in great athletic condition before the accident. Before the accident, my medical records stated that I had a "strong, muscular build." I worked out regularly. I also water-skied almost every day, sometimes twice a day, when I was in town. Unfortunately, the severe injuries, the grief, and the stress (not to mention the fabulously tasty hospital food) led to me losing over 30 pounds. And it was not just 30 pounds of fat; it was 30 pounds of functional muscle.

My sister's husband Shawn was the right man to help me get back into shape, along with my physical therapist. Shawn was in amazing physical condition, and he brought my weights and barbells into the, "Uh-oh" room. We called it that because of a funny story. Kelley and I decided to make that room the playroom, but there was a dining room table that had been sitting in that room for a while. When we moved the table, sharp depressions were left in the carpet. Little Laura, about a year old, squatted down to that spot on the carpet, pointed to the sunken dent, and said "uh-oh!" We all laughed because it was so cute. So after that, we affectionately called that room the "uh-oh!" room.

I decided that each day my main goal was to start building up the strength in my body, and I used those weights whenever I could. I soon had a physical therapist coming to my home to work with me. He was in his mid-50s and slender, with thinning hair. I will never forget Charlie, for reasons that are about to become apparent to you. When I first met him, he began his evaluation in the kitchen to see where I was at physically. He did a whole series of small tests. I knew I was in bad shape and had a long way to go, but I was not going to give up.

When I was in the hospital, the surgeons who reattached my feet told my sister and dad that I would likely never be able to walk on them again. They underestimated my will power. I don't like it when people tell me I can't do something. I guess that's the indomitable spirit that I inherited from my mother who, as you know, never gave up. Charlie asked me, "So, Joe, what is your goal in terms of physical therapy?" He had a snippy attitude and a condescending tone right off the bat. I told him that I wanted to get out of the wheelchair and walk. He gave me one of those looks.

You know the kind of look I'm talking about—that slow-eyed look that somebody gives you when he thinks you're slightly crazy and what you are saying is a little north of ridiculous? We have all had someone look at us in that infuriating manner. He turned away briefly, then looked back at me and, with a smirk on his face, said, "That sure is very optimistic, Joe, but I don't think you should have such high goals." So that was the end of poor old Charlie. (No, relax. It's not what you're thinking!) I didn't shoot him like Dirty Harry would have—that would be illegal in most states. What I did do is sit back in my chair and tell him to get out of my home and to never step foot into it ever again for the rest of his life. Charlie was quite shocked, but the delivery and the heat behind my message convinced him it would be a good idea to leave. The gall of that man!

Fortunately, my next home therapist was a wonderful man who I will never forget. His name was Kevin Kunkel. Kevin was a former college baseball player. He was in his mid-30s, had dirty blonde hair, was full of positive energy, and had a bright optimistic outlook on life. I liked him right away. Even though he never said it, I got the feeling that Kevin did not think it was his job to give me an opinion on whether I could or could not do something. He just said, "OK, let's get started." He believed in me, and I sensed that. This was the guy for me! After a couple of months of home therapy (two to three times a week), I made it to the next level, and I started going to Kevin's therapy clinic called Flagler Rehabilitation Center. Between my appointments with Kevin and lifting weights with Shawn at home, I was finally starting to make significant progress. My body got stronger every day.

I was positively motivated and confident that I was going to be back to normal and flying jets again one day. I am very grateful to Shawn for having spent so much time with me in my recovery. I worked hard to get from wheelchair to walker after only one month at home. I was kind of in a hurry, because I created a contract with myself. I was not going to have my sister shave me. My beard would have to grow until the day that I could stand by myself and shave on my own. I did not want other people having to go to the trouble of shaving me, and it was also a very motivating goal. I wanted to stand on my own two slightly-less-than-functional feet and shave.

I then graduated from walker to crutches with arm supports. Eventually, my balance and motor skills improved to the point where I was walking with two canes. I knew that if I was going to be back in the saddle again (flying), I had to keep progressing. Going backward was not an option. I was positively motivated to get my life back, even though the girls were not physically in it. I was always focused on improving just like I was when I competed in water and snow skiing competitions. Pushing for improvement is in my makeup, in my self-made DNA. Each baby step that I took led to another. That step told the one behind it "Let's go!"

In June of 1997, which was about seven months after D-day, I was walking really well with a walker. A sudden deep and severe depression snuck up on me, spread into my body, and brought a dark heaviness to my heart. I was completely surprised when this happened. Every day, several times a day, I would just sit sobbing. Maybe I never got the chance to grieve. After all, I missed my family's funeral. I hate to admit it now, but at that moment in my life, I truly, honestly wanted to die. I owned rifles and guns, and I had a loaded Smith & Wesson model 69 .44 Magnum.

You may remember this monstrously big pistol. It was the one proudly carried by Dirty Harry. I was sitting on my bed, and that gun was on my headboard, within arm's reach in case we ever had an uninvited intruder. I knew it was there. It was calling to me, making me aware of its presence. What do you think I did with it? Did I take it out of the headboard and hold it in my hand contemplating suicide? Did I stare at it and look down the barrel? Did I gingerly rub the barrel of the gun against the side of my temple? Did I play Russian roulette? *No. No. No!* It stayed where it was in the headboard and never came out. I kept it there because I was *not* going to take my own life.

But here is an admission from the bottom of my heart—I asked God to take me. I asked Him to take me away from the earth to be with my angels. I asked many, many times and prayed fervently, hoping it would happen. After a couple of weeks, the severe depression and the dark veil lifted. Apparently, God had some other special plan for me. I told God if He decided to keep me on earth that I would pledge to serve Him and help other people on the planet learn how to overcome their greatest adversities. This became my mission.

When I look back on my life, I was never a classically religious person. I think that my mom's overzealous pursuit of her religion may have turned me off. I ran away from religion in some ways. In my adult years, before the crash, I did not study the Bible or attend church. I was a Christian, but not one who was active in Christian worship or study. Some would describe me as a non-active Christian. I never really cared too much for labels; they're much too narrow and tend to create a stereotypical group that I never seem to fit in with. I was living and loving life, working, and having a good time. I really never gave religion too much of a thought. This changed for me in the hospital.

In the hospital, I would sob so hard that I felt like my body was going to burst from the exertion and pain. The pain was physically and mentally real. For some reason, I would cry out, "Lord, help me!" To my own amazement (OK, maybe I was somewhat of a skeptic), complete peace would come over me within 30 seconds. So I put two and two together and knew that there was something there in my heart. For every time I have called His name, the Prince of Peace brought me the gift of peace. No drug or rehab or surgical procedure could do that, only Him.

The sobbing lessened as my heart mended. I never felt the need to have therapy or to go to a support group for my grief. I know others find it helpful; it just wasn't for me. I was very blessed to have the strong support of my family and all my wonderful friends. I never took one pill for depression or anxiety. Ever. I do understand that some people experience great relief by taking antidepressants, and I would never fault anyone for that. I just didn't need them to get through my grief.

When I first got home, there were other areas of my life that were also a challenge. I started feeding myself, but I got a case of the "dropsies" for a while—I kept dropping food, plates, and glasses. Good thing it was something I could work on. That eventually went away. I also had to set aside my pride for a little while when I realized that cutting up food like meat and chicken was nearly impossible at first. Like a toddler, I had to have other people cut up my food. I could dress myself, but I really struggled at first because I still needed help with buttons. Overall, my sister and her family lived with and helped me for eight months. That was such a wonderful, selfless thing to do, and I will always be grateful for them and what they did.

I was also in a very fortunate financial situation because I was a US Airways captain. I knew that the contract would allow me to collect disability pay. I had known other pilots who had collected disability pay for different heart conditions. When my sick pay was used up in July of 1997, US Airways generously agreed to start paying me the monthly check for disability.

At this point in my life, I also became very curious about what caused the accident and whether someone or something was at fault. When I was in the rehab unit at St. Mary's hospital, my good friend Lee Thompson came to visit me. He was a fellow pilot who had a twin Bonanza plane that we used for the Flying Fez program to fly kids to various Shriners' hospitals. Additionally, Lee happened to be an attorney. He is the one who actually brought up the subject of a lawsuit when I was still in the hospital, and he did the initial research into whether a lawsuit was warranted or not. Lee Thompson is a good man, and he put in many hours of work on my case.

At around that same time, in July, the National Transportation Safety Board (NTSB) report came out, which found that the engine on the plane had failed due to a faulty part. The part was a spring-loaded door to the air box. A mechanic installed the part during a regularly scheduled annual inspection on the Bellanca Viking. The FAA had issued an Airworthiness Directive indicating that there was a known safety problem with that part. In other words, the mechanics who put that airbox on that plane were in direct violation of the FAA's warning. I was not at fault. That, of course, meant a lot to me.

I decided to file a lawsuit.

I was optimistic that my healing was happening and I would be back in the cockpit flying again. Not only was flying in my blood for the thrill, challenge, and adventure, but I always loved the freedom you feel when you are flying a piece of metal in the air, defying gravity. When my vision had improved to 20/40 on the left side and 20/50 on the right side, I tried different treatments to improve my vision further.

My vision was stagnating. It was not to be. It stopped improving. The other challenge I had with my vision is that it felt like I was holding onto a vibrating jackhammer. I still have this condition today. The jackhammer has reduced in size from industrial to a handheld. My vision is not blurry, but the image I am seeing is always shaking in small and rapid movements. This is a result of the brain injury, and I still have some damage in that area. The impairment in my eyes is called oscillopsia. It is described as follows:

> Oscillopsia is a visual disturbance in which objects in the visual field appear to oscillate. The severity of the effect may range from a mild blurring to rapid and periodic jumping. Oscillopsia may be caused by loss of the vestibulo-ocular reflex, involuntary eye movements such as nystagmus, or impaired coordination in the visual cortex (especially due to toxins) and is one of the symptoms of superior canal dehiscence syndrome. Sufferers may experience dizziness and nausea.[2]

But I can see! I just cannot see well enough to pass the stringent eye test requirements to be certified as a pilot. So I am grounded for now.

I am still hopeful to this day, after more than 14 years. The University of Colorado has a research program that I am hoping to be accepted into where patients who have this condition are treated with magnetic stimulation. They have seen positive results for my condition. So there is hope for that or future technology and developments.

After getting better physically and getting my finances handled, I still had to figure out what I was going to do with the rest of my life if I couldn't fly. I was still very lonely. I am not a loner nor have I ever been. I guess I am a "pack dog." I love being, *and have to be*, around people. I particularly always felt the need to have a mate, a partner, a woman. I couldn't ever see myself starring in a movie called *Joe: Alone*. That just wasn't me.

When Kelley was alive, she had always said she wanted me to be happy and remarry if something ever happened to her. Kelley had lost her best friend a few years before the accident, and she had broached the subject with me about remarriage after tragedy. I still remember the conversation. Kelley told me she did not want me to be alone in the event that anything happened to her. She wanted me to remarry. Somehow, I knew in my heart that it would one day happen. I was a *Soul Survivor* looking for my next soul mate.

"Joe, this is just an amazing story," I said to him.

"Thanks, but I didn't create it. I just lived it," he replied.

"I think that wraps up today. Let's talk again next week," I said.

"OK, buddy. Have a great day!" said Joe.

I hung up the phone and sat looking out my window. I thought about all that Joe had endured. Yet at the end of the call he said, "Have a great day." I think there is a lesson in that for all of us.

I looked out my window; I have perfect vision. None of the images shake. I have a wife in the next room whom I can go give a hug to if I take a break from writing. I have a beautiful daughter and a great son-in-law. I am blessed, but that word is so inadequate to describe how grateful I am for my life and the people in it.

Do we appreciate our blessings? Maybe more importantly, do we treat people we love as if they are a blessing to us? Do we let them know? Do we treat them like we should? We always read stories about people who, after losing someone close, say "I wish I would have…" (fill in the blank—loved him, kissed her, told them something). We can all learn from Joe's story to appreciate our loved ones even more. Bottom line: in a blink of an eye, our time on earth is over. Do we relish the time we have with others?

Endnotes

1. C.S. Lewis, quoted on *Thinkexist.com;* http://thinkexist.com/quotation/part_of_every_misery_is-so_to_speak-the_misery-s/325160.html; accessed May 19, 2011.

2. "Oscillopsia," *Wikipedia;* http://en.wikipedia.org/wiki/Oscillopsia; accessed May 19, 2011.

Chapter 8

Wasting Away in Recoveryville

Never let your head hang down. Never give up and sit down and grieve. Find another way. And don't pray when it rains if you don't pray when the sun shines.—Richard M. Nixon[1]

Over the next several weeks, Joe's story was always on my mind. I would find myself on a drive or out for a walk, and I would think of his life and of the crash. Is a crushing loss like losing your family like falling into a deep well? Do you recover really slowly until one day you reach the surface and break through? I can't imagine it, and it would be arrogant of anyone to think they could unless they had gone through it. I was curious to hear what Joe would have to say about it. I was feeling empathy and guilt in some ways that I had a family and hadn't had something like that happen to me. At the same time, I was feeling joy that Joe's story could finally be told. So I was looking forward to talking to my new friend yet again.

"Hey, Joe, how are you doing?" I said to Joe on our next phone call.

"I am doing *fantabulous!* I have been talking to lots of my friends about the book. They are all very excited and can't wait to read it," he said excitedly.

"Yes, I have the same response from my friends and family," I said.

"So what do we want to talk about today, Shawn?" Joe asked.

"I guess we are at the recovery phase. You have started recovering and are trying to figure out what is next, right?"

"Yep, that sounds right. So here goes."

So, after a very long time, I was now living on my own. It was also the first time since my adult married life had started that I was truly living alone. Even though I had lots and lots of family and friends who constantly visited me, I still felt the loss of my girls very deeply during that phase in my life. I was living alone in our big, rambling house on the lake. I would look out the window at the back of our house and see the lake that Kelley and I spent so many happy hours skiing on. I would think to myself, as I was watching television, *Oh, I have to make sure to tell Kelley about this show,* and then it would hit me like a ton of emotional bricks that Kelley was not around and that I would never be able to tell her.

I remember shopping at the grocery store and picking up a pack of cookies and thinking to myself, *The girls will really love these.* Then it would hit me like a bolt of lightning that the girls were not at home; in fact, they weren't anywhere on the earth. A song, a smell, a breeze, an expression that someone said, a picture could bring it all back and remind me that I was alone. When you live with a family for so long, this is a cruel trick your mind plays on you. I knew from a logical perspective that they were gone, but they were so much a part of my daily existence that they became part of me. They *were* me. I ate and drank and slept with my family, and suddenly they were yanked from my life. A part of me had died.

It was really hard for me in those passing days to imagine that happy times would ever return. I so desperately wanted to be completely well, but it was a huge challenge. My body was not only broken, but my heart was broken too. There was a Bee Gees song out several years ago that described how I was feeling:

> I can think of younger days when living for my life
> Was everything a man could want to do.
> I could never see tomorrow, but I was never told about
> the sorrow.
>
> And how can you mend a broken heart?
> How can you stop the rain from falling down?
> How can you stop the sun from shining?
> What makes the world go round?
> How can you mend this broken man?
> How can a loser ever win?
> Please help me mend my broken heart and let me live
> again.
>
> I can still feel the breeze that rustles through the trees
> And misty memories of days gone by
> We could never see tomorrow, no one said a word about
> the sorrow.
>
> And how can you mend a broken heart
> How can you stop the rain from falling down?
> How can you stop the sun from shining?
> What makes the world go round?
> How can you mend this broken man?
> How can a loser ever win.[2]

I don't know if all the friends who came to cheer me up know how much they helped. So many of them visited so often, and they were so loyal to me. I felt the love pouring out of them. They often say that you do not know how many friends you have, and I found that to be true. I found the opposite of what that saying implies; I found I had more friends than I ever imagined possible. I do know this; I am fully convinced I would not be here today if it wasn't for the love and loyalty and diligence of my family and friends. See, I not only have loving and wonderful friends, but I also have stubborn friends, and they just were not going to give up on me or allow me to give up on myself. I am so blessed.

During that period of my life, I stayed in touch with the nurse from the hospital in Georgia. Her name was Tara. She was very similar in character to Kelley in that she was the loving, caring, nurturing type. We developed a strong friendship after she called me the first time in West Palm to see how I was doing. She came to visit me in West Palm, and I went to visit her several times in Albany. We enjoyed each other's company, and we both had a similar outlook on life. She made me smile.

Some may read this and judge me for striking up a friendship with another woman so soon after losing my wife. I do not have to defend myself; I had been through a lot. I loved Kelley, and nothing would replace her, but even Kelley would have wanted me to move on. I was lonely and I needed a female friend. I'm sure any Hollywood screenwriter could have predicted what would happen next. Like me, Tara had two daughters (from a previous marriage), and she was a great mother. When I saw her around her children, I could see her love beaming for them as well as for the rest of her family. She was smart, pretty, and loved life. Slowly over time, my feelings for Tara developed into something much deeper, and for the first time since the accident, I started to feel happier. I started to have thoughts and entertain the idea of possibly remarrying, which surprised even me.

I asked Tara about marriage. At first she really liked the idea. When she had time to think about it more, over a period of a couple weeks, she told me that I was still grieving for Kelley and my girls. As painful as it was for her, she said that I needed more time to heal emotionally before I could start a life together with someone else. At the time I did not agree, and I was baffled. But looking back through the lens of history, I see that Tara was very mature and very wise in seeing that I needed time alone to grieve. She was right. This was a true act of love and unselfishness, as she made sure that my needs were taken care of first, before hers. I also think that she sensed that a marriage so soon after the accident would not have been successful and would have led to more pain in both of our lives. We remained very close friends, and she still visited occasionally, but the topic of marriage never came up again.

Gradually, my physical and occupational therapy sessions got to be fewer and fewer. I spent less time around Kevin and, even though I thought he was a great guy, I was ready to move to the next phase of my life. I was making significant improvements in my health and recovery. I sat down and developed my own recovery plan (I called it the Townsend method!), which included walking around the neighborhood, swimming in the pool with my ski vest on (so I would not drown), and weightlifting. I decided that if I was going to make any further progress in my recovery, it was going to be up to me.

I also came up with a plan to take my walks around the neighborhood. When would I take these walks? I was no dummy, so I took my walk at just about dinnertime. It was a 1.7-mile loop that I would usually walk twice in order to build up my appetite. I would, of course, stop by several great neighbors' houses, and they would coincidentally invite me in to join them for dinner. Of course, I would protest mildly and then accept their invitation. It was a great comfort to me to have good food, but more importantly, it also fed my gnawing sense of loneliness. (My evil plan worked!) All of those wonderful people know who they are, and their love and support was a true blessing for me in those lonely days. I was so lucky to have great neighbors. I come from a big family, and we often had family dinners at my sisters' and parents' homes, so I felt the love there as well. For me, food has always been part of love, and love has always been part of food.

Kelley's parents lived an hour north, and I would occasionally go and spend the weekend with them. After all, they have been my in-laws for many years. Kelley's mom was also a great cook. When I was in the hospital, she would pick up my dirty laundry and bring it back to me clean the next day. (I wasn't going to wear those goofy gowns for so long.) I was always appreciative of her kindness at that time.

As I mentioned in the last chapter, Lee Thompson had come to visit me in the hospital, and after all due diligence, I decided to file a lawsuit. Now to be clear, I am not the kind of person who believes you should sue someone for minor infractions. I think we all sue too much and too often. But what happened to my family was life-shattering and huge, and I could not ignore it. The facts were true and brutal—all because of a negligent mechanic, who did not bother to read the Air Worthiness Directive concerning the air box he installed. The plane I was flying crashed and killed my family. So I entered the lawsuit after much thought and much soul-searching to determine if it was really something I should do. So as the saying goes, I "lawyered up" to begin a fight with the insurance company of the aviation services people. I had to. At the time, my injuries were so severe and my expenses were so great, I was worried that I might end up homeless. After all, health plans all have limitations and only pay for certain things. At some point, those benefits would run out. Then where would I be?

Lee had suggested that I use an attorney who specialized in airplane accidents. He introduced me to Steve Marks in Miami. It took a very long time to get a trial date, but eventually we had a trial date in Tampa, Florida. Two weeks before the trial, I had one of many reconstructive surgeries on my feet, and I was back in a wheelchair. Kelley's parents were kind enough to drive me over to Tampa for the trial, where I met the mechanic who was at fault. I was in a wheelchair at that time, and had my foot in a cast as I was recovering from another of my many reconstructive surgeries. As they say, the wheels of justice turn slowly. Then they came to a screeching halt. There was a problem with the jury, and the trial had to be postponed. Dealing with the attorneys for the insurance company was a game of cat and mouse. Several months later, the cat blinked. The defense offered a cash settlement in the low seven figures. I accepted and received a nice, big, fat check after the attorneys got their share.

So now, a few years after D-Day, I had in my possession a big fat check written by Witmer Aviation's insurance company. Getting a check like that is like the best of times and the worst of times. Part of you is delighted that justice was served and that the bad guy had to pay. You are relieved to have the money. You feel more secure. At the same time, the bigger part of you wishes none of this had ever happened. I would gladly give the check back to have my family restored. Another interesting aspect about having money (lots of it) is that everyone was suddenly my friend, especially Kelley's family.

I became a greed magnet. They never said it, but I always sensed that they thought that part of the money was justifiably theirs. I also think they wanted to play on my guilt (even though it had been proven that the accident was not my fault) to get their share of equity. Kelley's brother had designed a great 34-foot open fisherman boat. He started a boat company, A1A Nautical Incorporated. Kelley's family sat down and asked me to be a silent investor in the company. When I originally bought into the company, there were two other investors, but as time went on, I bought them out and became the sole owner of A1A Nautical, Inc. It was a huge undertaking, but I was willing to do it for Kelley's family. In order to build a new model boat, you have to build plugs, then molds, then the actual fiberglass boat.

They say that timing is everything, and unfortunately when September 11 hit, it also hit the economy like a bomb. The disposable income for boat buyers just dried up. Due in part to lack of business insight and strategy, the company faltered. He was only selling boats factory direct and not through a network of dealers. It was like having one salesperson instead of hundreds. Who do you think was funding all of the operations and salary? The Joe Townsend National Bank, that's who!

I was using my blood money. This is not their description; it is mine and mine alone. I call it blood money because it came from a result of all of the spilled blood. I was paying out as much as $50,000 plus per month, and the company was swimming in a sea of red ink, as we had never turned a profit. The boat company began to die. There were a couple of buyers interested in buying the company from me for about $400,000. That would have been a loss of over $1 million dollars, but something was certainly better than nothing.

Kelley's brother, however, never fully cooperated with that plan. What did he do? First, he wanted a huge paycheck to stay on as manager of the company. He also relocated the boat molds to a location unknown to me. If you are buying a boat manufacturing company, you need the boat molds. These boat molds were the primary asset of the company, so the buyers changed their minds and walked away. It's pretty hard to make a boat out of fiberglass if there are no molds. I asked him where the boat molds were, and he finally confessed that they had been stored on a property in Fort Pierce. A friend of mine later told me that the molds were never there; and, in fact, to this day, I am still not sure what happened to them.

Now that I had no buyers left and no money left, he added insult to injury by faxing me a purchase contract to buy the company from me for a whopping $5,000! Why would I sell a company that was worth $400,000 (with the molds) for $5,000? After he cost me well over $1 million and the opportunity to recoup $400,000, there was *no* way I was going to let him walk all over me and sell the company to him for a pittance and give him a good laugh. So his idea to hoodwink his late sister's husband and make me look like a sap never happened. I would rather have lost the shirt off my back then to let him humiliate me any longer. He had already turned me into the biggest sucker that he could by drawing my blood money from me.

Now that my fortune was lost at sea, I had to make changes. Sadly, I had to sell the beautiful lakefront home that I had built with Kelley. Now that I was no longer able to fund the boat company and all I had left was my good looks, Kelley's family abandoned me as their son and as their brother-in-law. The Bible says that the love of money is the root of all kinds of evil (see 1 Tim. 6:10). The *love* of money is evil, and when people love money too much, they will do evil things to get it. It is unfortunately true that money will bring out the true character in a person.

It seems appropriate that Kelley's family were done with me after they had helped drain me of my blood money. They talked to an attorney early on to see about a lawsuit, and they were told that I was the only person whom they could sue so they decided not to proceed with any litigation. Maybe it was just the natural progression of things, or maybe it was something more, but my relationship with Kelley's family came to an end.

So now I had lost my family (Kelley and the girls), most of my money, my house, and all of Kelley's family. I was lost. My only anchor was my friends, my parents, and my sisters; so I hung onto them for dear life. They were my life preserver in an ocean of loneliness.

Does life pile on? Why is it that some people never face much adversity and others get way more than they deserve? I don't know. Joe faced everything else, but on top of all of this winning a settlement and then, in the curve ball that life throws, losing a large percentage of it in a family business. This seems like just way too much for one person to bear. Yet despite that entire sad tale, Joe remains positive upbeat and optimistic. That to me is amazing and something everyone can learn from. I believe it isn't what happens to us that matters; it is how we respond to what happens to us. Joe could be mean and bitter, and some people would even give him permission to be. Joe chooses not to be, but to overcome instead. He is Tigger—he just bounces. That we can all learn from.

"Wow, Joe. I am sorry they were so cruel to you."

"I am too, Shawn."

"I guess there are people like that in the world," I said. "I just wish, sometimes, that there didn't have to be."

"Me too," he replied.

"So when do we talk next, Joe?" I asked.

"Well, there is a possibility we may be coming through Philly on a trip in the next few weeks. I will let you know," he said.

"Thanks, Captain."

"Sure thing, buddy!" Joe said as he hung up the phone.

ENDNOTES

1. Richard M. Nixon, quoted on *Brainy Quote;* http://www.brainyquote.com/quotes/quotes/r/richardmn120433.html; accessed May 19, 2011.

2. The Bee Gees, "How Can You Mend a Broken Heart," *Trafalgar* (1971).

Chapter 9

The Fork in the Road

The most precious possession that ever comes to a man in this world is a woman's heart.—Josiah G. Holland[1]

My phone rang in my office.

"Hey, Shawn."

"Hey, Captain Joe. What is going on, Joseppy?"

"Well, Carol and I are going on a trip, and we can swing through Philly and then you can meet her. Would you like that?"

"I would love that, Joe," I said.

"Oh good," he said. "She wants to meet you, too."

We arranged a day and a time, and I was looking forward to meeting Carol. She was everything Joe said she was. She was warm, beautiful, and had a great sense of humor.

I picked them up and took them into the city. Joe wanted to get a cheese steak sandwich, as Carol had never had one. We asked several people what kind of cheese was the official cheese steak cheese. There was hot debate over whether it was provolone or Cheez Whiz®. Only in Philly would anyone have this conversation.

We sat down at our table with our way-too-big sandwiches.

"Well," I said, "I am so happy to meet you, Carol. This is perfect because Joe is going to talk to me today about dating and marriage, so please share your thoughts as well."

"Yes, honey," Joe said to Carol. "Please add anything I leave out."

Carol looked over at Joe lovingly and said, "Will do."

"OK, Joe, let's get started," I said smiling at both of them.

I am a very blessed man in many ways. I have also been blessed in my life with some wonderful female companions. I have dated some of them, and I have married some of them. All of them were not only gorgeous looking on the outside, but also even more beautiful on the inside. I think because I have such admiration and respect for women, women return that level of respect to me.

The next woman who had an influence on my life after Tara was Gloria. I met Gloria Tanner at the most romantic of places, a mutual friend's wedding. After all, when people meet at a wedding, they are already in a romantic mindset and are also dressed up in their nicest duds. Gloria and I became friends and began to date for over a year. Gloria was 5 feet 8 inches with blond hair and blue eyes, and she was very attractive. She worked as a bookkeeper for Pax television, a family television network. She was a very happy person, very consoling, and wanted to please me with her kindness.

She was there to read for me as well when I would wobble. We even went to Russia together to share our love with children in large foster homes and in a boy's prison. Gloria was beautiful and gifted at writing poetry, and wrote me a very touching poem. I had never had anyone write a poem just for me. If you think about the time, the energy, and the effort that goes into writing a poem for one person, it is pretty humbling.

JOE'S FLIGHT TO AMAZING GRACE

In a split second they were gone,
The plane crash took all that I held dear,
Never got a chance to say goodbye,
Just left alone and my heartache and tears.

I was there too—I should have died,
For a short time I did.
I saw no bright lights or Jesus' face,
It was hell I visited.

God in His mercy gave me a second chance,
And He breathed life back into me.
Even though recovery is so hard,
There is triumph in this tragedy.

My body was broken and battered,
I couldn't walk and couldn't see,
But the physical pain could never compare,
To losing my sweet Angels Laura, Tara, and Kelley.

One day a neighbor stopped by,
Said there was a choice I needed to make,
If I wanted to see my three angels again,
In my heart Jesus I'd need to take.

So he led me in the sinner's prayer,

And put my life into God's hands,
He's continually healing my body and soul,
And revealing to me His purpose and plans.

I used to fly the wind of my own strength,
Now God's love is what I embrace,
And that is the wind that carries me,
On this flight of Amazing Grace.

Gloria was a great gal who was very loving and kindhearted, and I foolishly did not realize at the time how great she was. I guess I took her for granted by not giving her my full attention. When she realized that, our relationship did not survive. I was the insensitive meathead in this situation, and when I realized it, it was too late to recover. Once she was gone, and we were no longer dating, I was seriously brokenhearted over being foolish and losing Gloria. If I could speak to her now, I would apologize for waiting too long to notice that she truly loved me and that I had not returned the feelings. For that, I am truly sorry.

My life changed forever when I met an amazing woman named Carol. My good friends, Steve and Debbie Boswell, came to visit in March of 2001. They were in town for a friend's surprise birthday party. I met Steve through my buddy, Joey Piazza, who I flew with at BizJet. You know, for some reason women are just great matchmakers. Even in movies all of the great matchmakers are women. So I believe there's some truth to that. What is especially funny is the way women go about matching people up and the psychology they use by asking casual questions.

My friend Debbie said, "So, Joe, would you be interested in meeting one of my friends? You would really like her." She actually offered me two choices; she had two friends to pick from. Pick door number 1 or door number 2. She was my dating Monty Hall, the longtime host of *Let's Make a Deal*. I asked where they each lived. She said that one lived in California and one lived in Colorado. Asking her valued opinion, I inquired as to which one she thought I should call first. She immediately said that she thought I should call Carol first.

She had given Carol a copy of the short version of my story to read because Carol had been through a bad breakup with her ex-husband and was feeling down. She had been married for over seven years, but unfortunately things did not work out. Ironically, Carol had written in her journal a while before Debbie gave her my story that she would "like to meet a widower someday who had lost his love partner and might be ready to try again." After Carol read my ten-page short story, she told several people that she would like to meet someone "like that Joe Townsend." I don't know why, but the story just connected to her heart. She really had no reason to believe that she would ever meet Joe Townsend. After all, Carol lived in Denver, Colorado, and I was 2,000 miles away in Florida.

On April 6, 2001, I gave Carol a call. I really liked how she sounded on the phone. (I can't explain it much better than that; she just sounded really nice. How lame does that sound?) As it turns out, we ended up talking on the phone for a couple of hours. When talking to her, for some reason, I felt like I had known her for a long time. The conversation flowed easily, and we never seemed to run out of things to talk about. The time just seemed to fly by, and we couldn't believe that we had talked for that long.

Carol is a very happy person and an excellent storyteller (a trait she inherited from her father). She could keep me entertained on the phone for hours. I remember vividly a song released back then called "I Knew I Loved You" by the band Savage Garden, because it talks about loving a person before you know them. It became one of "our" songs. I called her again the next night, and we talked for a couple of hours again. We were also able to share our faith on our calls across the US from east to west. Sadly this was not something that Kelley and I shared, because back then my faith was only in me. We discovered that we both loved to travel and that we were both moderate in our political beliefs. We kept calling the next night, and the next night, and the next night. Hmmm. A pattern was definitely developing here, and it was a pattern that I recognized. We had a magic chemistry even over the phone. It doesn't take me too long to catch on. So after a few weeks, I flew from Florida to Colorado to meet the amazing Carol in person. I was floored by how beautiful she was, and our chemistry multiplied by ten in person.

We have amazing differences, but we complement one another pretty well. Carol is a neat person, or as some would say a neatnik. I am not. Carol is detail-oriented, and I see the big picture. I am extremely gregarious and thrive in groups of people large or small, and Carol is much more comfortable in the company of one or two people. She would never want to be the center of attention, and I have never minded being in that position. So we are a perfect match of commonalities and complementary opposites. Her strengths made up for my weak points and vice versa.

The other thing that amazed me is that she was not cautious with me or overly protective, despite what she went through in her first marriage. I mean, who could not love my warm heart, good looks, and that great Townsend smile? I remember asking my Mom when I was growing up, "How will I know when I am in love?" Her classic answer, used by parents worldwide, was the "Oh, you will just know." As soon as I saw Carol, I just knew. After only three weeks, I knew that I was going to ask her to marry me. It was a classic love-at-first-sight story, but in this case it was love at first phone call.

I had never dated a drug dealer before, so that was a unique experience for me. Don't be concerned; Carol was a drug dealer, but a legal one, working for a large pharmaceutical company called GlaxoSmithKline. Carol had won a sales contest and a trip to Grand Cayman and she had originally asked Debbie to go with her. Debbie gave her spot to me. I seized the opportunity, and that was when I began to plan the big surprise. This plan would surprise Carol and change both our lives.

I was to meet Carol in Miami to fly to Grand Cayman on American Airlines. Her company had generously provided the tickets. A very good friend of mine, JD, was a pilot for American, so I asked him if he could find out who was piloting our flight out of Miami. He said he knew one of the pilots, and that set my top-secret plan in motion. JD told his buddy, Adam, that I wanted to propose to Carol in the cockpit of the B-727, which is the aircraft that I first flew at Piedmont Airlines. Adam was expecting me in the gate area and, although we had never met, we were going to pretend that we were friends from flying private jets together. (Maybe I should have been in the CIA. I am kind of devious in making these kinds of plans!)

He invited us down to the aircraft cockpit before the boarding process began. As I was pointing out the flight engineer panel to Carol, I snuck the ring out of my pocket, opened the box, and asked her to marry me. She was floored to say the least and said with an excited tone, "OH, YES, YES!!!!" as I slipped the ring on her finger. It was a beautiful ring. It had a large heart-shaped diamond in the middle with a sparkling, smaller diamond on each side of the heart. Based on her reaction, I seem to have picked the ring well. At that point, we had known one another for just one month.

First Officer Adam was smiling ear to ear, snapped a picture of us with our camera, and then seated us in first class with a bottle of champagne. The next four days in Grand Cayman were a blast. We went sailing to an area that was home to stingrays. We snorkeled in the clear, blue water watching the elegant stingrays glide through their space, as if they were flying. We went on a submarine dive over the edge of a reef and dropped to a very deep level. We went on a Sea-Doo® jet ski around the harbor one day and participated in an amazing scavenger hunt all over the island using jeeps provided by the company. On the last night, there was a great barbecue outside on the beach with the sunset, white sand, and Jamaican jerk pork and chicken. It was the trip of a lifetime. We flew back to Miami and drove to my home in West Palm Beach for a couple of days until my fiancée had to fly back to Denver.

A while after I had asked Carol to marry me, she offered to work full-time instead of part-time to help support us financially. What an amazing woman! What an amazing person! Carol had no idea of the financial settlements that I had received or would receive. (Carol and I met and married before I lost everything.) She, unlike many others, was not after anything except my heart. I was so touched that she was prepared to work full-time as a pharmaceutical rep in order to take care of me. You know, sometimes it's not what people say, but what they do, that lets you know that they truly love you. Carol loves me, but more importantly, Carol *is* *love*. I was also marrying a mom with two kids; Dave was 13 and Lisa was 8 years old. So, in a way, if I could not have a family, I was going to marry one. I was very blessed that both children were very supportive of me marrying their mom.

We picked September 21, 2001, to get married. I had purchased airline tickets, as I did not want to risk getting bumped as an airline employee on a stand-by pass. So the reservations were made. We had our simple and romantic wedding planned out, and the plan was to be married on the beach on Kauai in Hawaii. We had convertible rental cars booked, a fabulous hotel, a wonderful preacher, a luau, and the grand finale, a four-wheeler picnic ride through the forest. Then, as the saying goes, "all heck broke loose!" and the world stopped spinning. Right about that time, some evil terrorist decided to take control of a few airplanes. Two planes crashed into the World Trade Center and the Pentagon, but not somewhere else, because the brave passengers of United flight 93 (of "Let's roll!" fame) fought back and crashed the plane in a lonely field in Pennsylvania.

So how were the wedding guests and wedding party going to get to Hawaii? Good question. Well, the answer is that they were going to fly on a plane. As you may remember, for about a week after 9/11, all air travel came to a complete halt. After that, air travel resumed, and we still could have made it easily to Hawaii and have had a great time. Carol and I were ready to fly, and we would have. However, our guests were not too pleased with that idea. I had asked Kelley's brother to be my best man, and I agreed to buy him and his family airline tickets, pay all the expenses for a rental van, hotel meals, and all the works. At the time, I could afford to do this because the blood money was plentiful. The boat business had not failed at this point, and we were still on great terms. I also invited Kelley's mom and dad on an all-expenses paid vacation to the wedding.

Carol and I were not afraid to fly after air travel resumed. In fact, it was probably the very safest time to fly because security had been enhanced dramatically. However, Kelley's mom would not step one foot on an airplane. I felt connected to Kelley's mom because, after all, she had been my mother-in-law for many years. We had always had a great relationship, and I looked at her as a mother figure. She could be very warm and loving, and that was something that I craved. After the accident, she had made it a point to stay in my life, and I felt a loyalty to her at the time. I just couldn't have a wedding without Kelley's mom present. The fact that she wouldn't fly threw a huge monkey wrench into our plans for a Hawaiian wedding. So our plans had to change quickly. Instead of getting married in Hawaii, we were married in the town of Baskin, Louisiana, a charming one-caution-light town. We were fortunate that Carol's Aunt Pauline was able to get us into her Baptist Church on short notice. Of course, we had a pretty good "excuse" for our sudden re-planning!

We got married at Baskin Baptist Church, a beautiful country church with a white clapboard exterior and a traditional, old-fashioned steeple. By most city standards, the church would be considered small, but it was charming, beautiful, and quaint. Several generations of Carol's family had attended church there, including her grandparents and mother, so it had a special meaning for the family. At that point, Carol's parents were living in nearby Monroe, Louisiana, and her brother was living close by in Jackson, Mississippi. I also had cousins from Arkansas who lived only an hour away, so they were able to attend as well.

Looking back on it, I should have picked another guy to be my best man instead of Kelley's brother. I could have chosen one of my friends or my brother-in-law, Shawn, who worked and lived with me after I got home from the hospital for over nine months. I have several other friends who would have all been honored to have been my best man. But at the time, I knew what I knew, and I did what I did, and that was before everything blew up at the boat company.

Carol came down the aisle wearing a long, white, fitted sun dress with spaghetti straps, and she was carrying a small bouquet of colorful wild flowers that we had purchased at a local florist. Carol's matron of honor was Debbie Boswell, the woman who was responsible for us meeting. She wore a blue, one-shouldered, short Hawaiian print dress. Carol's cousin, Bernard, was a local pastor and conducted the wedding for us. He was about our age with light-colored hair, a pleasant smile, and the demeanor of a true Southern gentleman. We had written our own vows and gave them to Bernard. He liked them so much he asked if he could keep them, and we were very honored and flattered and said, "Of course."

The reception after the wedding was held in the church's fellowship hall, and Carol's Aunt Pauline had been nice enough to do most of the planning on our behalf since she lived there locally. We had about 30 people there, which surprised us because we didn't know how many people would show up. We were delighted that so many people came on such short notice. We played the Beatles song "All You Need is Love," and while it was playing, I remember thinking how very true that is. I did not think of Kelley at all that day because I felt it was Carol's day, and I wanted it to be all hers.

Thurman Dickey catered our wedding, and he prepared an amazing BBQ chicken dinner with all of the various side dishes. It was an incredible feast topped off with the best carrot cake I have ever eaten. It is fair to say it was an incredible day.

A few weeks later, we had a second wedding reception in West Palm Beach for all of my Florida friends. There were over 200 friends and family members who attended. In a twist of irony, we had the reception at St. Peter's United Methodist Church, the very same church where the funeral was held for my girls. We had a reception in the fellowship hall, and it was a Hawaiian themed party. We had our second amazing BBQ dinner and could not resist having another carrot cake just like the one we had in Louisiana. A friend of mine, Ed Schaeffer, volunteered to decorate the fellowship hall in a Hawaiian motif, and it was no surprise that he did a great job. The room was decorated with coconuts and tiki lights, and everybody received a plastic Hawaiian lei. We had asked everyone to wear Hawaiian tropical clothing, and they did. To my delight, Kelley's mom and dad attended both events in Louisiana and West Palm.

Instead of honeymooning in Hawaii, we had our honeymoon in Natchez, Mississippi, and stayed at the wonderful and beautiful Monmouth Plantation. The Monmouth was a Southern plantation once owned by General John Quitman, and this antebellum house and grounds are filled with every luxurious detail. The grounds had walking paths and beautiful gardens. When we drove up the driveway to the front entrance to the Monmouth, we felt like we had arrived at Tara (the house in *Gone with the Wind*). We always felt like we should sit outside on the porch and have mint juleps. One night we had a fabulous gourmet dinner that we shared with several other guests, and the next day was the finest breakfast buffet that I have ever seen. It had fantastic grits, eggs, and amazing fresh fruit. It was not Hawaii, but it was a special place, and we started our life together in a wonderful Southern mansion. In life, you can either let surprises upset you, or you can roll with the punches and just go with plan B. Carol and I are both ready to roll with the punches. That's one of the things I love about her.

We left Natchez and decided to stop in New Orleans on the way back. We walked down Bourbon Street, which was a very eerie experience because it was just after 9/11 and there were no tourists there except for us. It was a Cajun ghost town. As a pilot, I had been there many times on layovers, and I expected to see crazy people dancing in the street. We enjoyed a delicious Cajun dinner and departed after being there for one night.

In Arlington, a suburb of Dallas, we stopped and visited my sweet Aunt Haley, who had raised my father. She was a great hostess and very funny. She loved Carol's personality, and she also loved Carol's toe ring and thought she would look good with one. At that time, Aunt Haley was almost 90 years old. She made the best sourdough bread I have ever tasted in a cast-iron skillet. We very much appreciated her old time, Southern hospitality and kissed her goodbye the next morning to head home. She and Carol became fast friends.

We had a grand time in both cities and decided to head back to Denver. I am a retired pilot, and I never get lost. This time, however, I had my new bride with me, and we were deliriously happy, and I guess distracted. We were driving north on I-35, and there was a fork where you could go to Salina, Kansas, on I-70. We were not paying attention and took the fork to Kansas City, Kansas, and added several hundred miles to our trip. This is like a pilot planning to land in Cleveland and landing in Cincinnati instead. We laughed it off and stayed at a roadside motel that night.

The next day we would drive up to I-70 West, which would actually take us to Denver. We were looking for a place to eat lunch. We stumbled upon the Coyote Café. It was a steakhouse with a salad bar, a potato bar, and a dessert bar. It's funny that some of your best, most meaningful moments are a result of just being spontaneous and going with the flow. We were there after the lunch rush, so the waitress was visiting with us. She was about 5 foot 4 inches tall with a slender body and shoulder-length brown hair. She looked like she had lived a hard life. You know what I mean; some people just have that look.

We could tell that she was upset. When we asked her, she told us her mother had been wrongly arrested because a neighbor's kid had stored drugs in her mother's shed. Her mother was unable to make her mobile home payment of $200 and, because of her situation, was probably going to lose her home. It just so happened that I had exactly $200 cash in my pocket. With Carol's support, I gave the waitress the money from my pocket so her mother would not lose her home. The waitress was so stunned she had to sit down, and she broke into tears and sobbed. She couldn't believe that a stranger would just walk in off the street and help without strings attached and give her mom such a blessing. That was a wonderful, poignant moment for Carol and me, and I was happy to share joy with that waitress. It is so much fun to do something for someone who least expects it and deserves it the most. None of us had a dry eye at that moment. Sure, I like to receive, but I believe that it is more of a blessing to give than it is to receive.

On our honeymoon, we talked about where we were going to live when we got back, because after all, I had a home in Florida, and Carol had a home in Colorado. We decided it would be best to stay in Colorado until Lisa was off to college and on her own. Since then, we have made so many good friends in our church and in our SSR club that we have decided to keep our two homes and spend summers in Denver and winters in Florida for obvious meteorological reasons. Neither one of us enjoys shoveling snow. It's a great lifestyle, and I feel blessed that it is possible.

Carol was working for GlaxoSmithKline part-time when we met. My disability income from US Air was enough to support us, so I gave her the option of quitting. She liked the idea that we had free travel benefits with US Airways that we could take advantage of as a couple. The part-time job would have been a hindrance to our travels, so Carol happily resigned from her job two months after we married.

Initially our marriage was a very easy, breezy time, as most marriages start out. That lasted about two years, and then out of the blue, I hit an emotional brick wall. I was questioning my decision to remarry, and we went through a very rough time, which was all because of me. Sometimes emotions are like a box, but when you open the box there's another box inside, and another one inside that one. Kind of like those sets of Russian dolls. I had not fully sorted through the emotions that I had boxed away. I felt crushing survivor guilt and, on top of that, the guilt of moving on with my life and not being able to share anything with Kelley. I was very emotionally distant from Carol during those two hard years, and I know I caused her a great deal of heartache.

I would escape to our home in Florida and spend an unusually large amount of time there while she was back in Colorado. To be brutally honest, I am not sure why Carol hung in there with me during the time I was being a big knucklehead, but she did. It took about two years to get to the other side of the emotional chasm, and I am grateful now that she was so committed to me and to our marriage. She was so incredibly patient. Our life together today is great.

The other aspect of Carol's personality that I dearly love is her level of empathy for anything and anyone who is suffering. She has always understood the horrific loss of my angels and has often said she's not sure she could go on if she lost her spouse and children in a flash. Carol is an avid reader, and she once read a book that claimed that someone was really teleported to another place. She was furious; she cannot stand writers who make stuff up that can't really happen (with apologies to Star Trek fans worldwide). That same night, she looked into my eyes and said, with a gentle smile, that if teleporting and time travel were truly possible, she would want me to go back in time and reunite with Kelley and my girls. She said this honestly from her heart without flinching, even though that would mean she would no longer be part of my life.

She definitely understands the intense depth of my pain. Her only frustration comes with knowing that she cannot do much about it, except support me. It can't be taken away. She doesn't begrudge me my first family. She knows that they lived, and she honors them. Every now and then, on a certain day, at a certain time, she will feel like she is the consolation prize, or second place, or the one I didn't choose first. (Carol said it was OK for me to say this.) I am obviously not a woman, but I think at times it would be hard for anyone to fill that role. Carol is my rock, and I love her for that.

We both love to take advantage of the free travel my airline disability provides us with and have been on many fun trips. London was the first European destination that we visited together as a couple. I had been there as a pilot on a layover when I was flying Learjets, but I never really got to see much. Carol had been to London a number of times and has often said, "You can never get enough of London." When you fly to Europe from the U.S., you generally leave at night and arrive the next morning. When we arrived in London, we decided to go on a tour bus so we wouldn't have to walk around in the chilly weather. The funny thing is, as soon as we got on board the warm, cozy tour bus with wonderful, comfortable seats, we both fell asleep and didn't see a thing. We had a great nap. One of our mutual interests is the history of World War II, and there is no better place to explore that era of time than England. We loved the fighting spirit of Winston Churchill and really enjoyed touring the many war-related museums in London. Our favorite was the Churchill Museum and Cabinet War Rooms, which was an underground bunker where Churchill bravely led the war efforts.

France was an interesting vacation because it was the one place in Europe where we decided to rent a car. It is also the last time Carol thinks we will do such a stupid thing. (I guess I agree.) We rented a five-speed Opel, which is a fun little car, but the traffic in Paris was a little hectic to say the least. We had the opportunity to drive to northern France and tour the Normandy region. It was awe-inspiring and beautiful. We took a tour of the beaches and the American cemetery and were never so proud to be Americans. We were there in December, so it was extremely cold and damp on the coast.

When we walked on the world famous Omaha Beach, we were the only ones there. It was a very humbling and haunting experience to be on the beach, look up, see the gun turrets, and to imagine all of those young Americans running out of the surf straight into the line of fire. It reminded me of a disturbing and truthful scene in *Saving Private Ryan* that depicted this event. Normandy was the one place in France where we saw American flags flying over homes there. The U.S. soldiers saved them from the tyranny of the Nazis. At the American cemetery, we were again humbled by the sacrifices made by so many. Our French tour guide told us that every grave had been adopted by a local family who put fresh flowers on the graves at different times throughout the year.

We have also been to Rome and San Diego. We explored all over the Wild West in Wyoming, Yellowstone, Yuma, and the Grand Canyon. We have stood on the corner in Winslow, Arizona, which was quite a sight to see. We have also been to Asheville, the Outer Banks, New York, and

Memphis. You know the commercial that says, "I'm an everywhere man"? I guess we are an "everywhere couple." We both love to see the sights, and it's wonderful sharing those experiences with someone you love.

I am very grateful to Carol for many reasons. One of the reasons is that she is always there with a shoulder to lean on, and I don't mean emotionally; I mean physically. (Well OK, emotionally too.) Due to the accident, I have a poor sense of balance, and I have shaky vision. She is always there to lean on at every curb, every step, every stair, and she will patiently read to me from a menu, the mail, or the bottom screen crawl on the news channel.

Despite my accident, I still have a passion for beautiful, speedy vehicles. It doesn't matter whether it's a train, a plane, or an automobile. I have always had a love for cars, and I fell in love with the Chevy SSR. It's just a cool retro-looking truck. Remember that I went retro in high school with my hot rod 1945 Willys Sedan Delivery. Carol has encouraged me, and the Lord has blessed me, with two cool, final production run Chevy SSRs. What is even cooler is that my brother-in-law, Douglas Ungematch, married to my sister Margarita, designed the SSR. Isn't that amazing? So that's all the more reason to think that it is cool.

The SSR is a two-seat, high-performance, retractable, hardtop convertible on a Trail Blazer chassis with a Corvette LS2 engine. Sorry for getting technical on you, but if the Corvette engine does not mean anything to you, just know that this truck kicks some major butt. There are close to 400 wild horses of horsepower under the hood.

The morning that my mother was taking her last breath, I got a chance to test this roaster out. My sisters called me at 3 AM from her bedside to say, "The time is near." Before I tell you what I did, I want to caution you to never try this at home. What I did was exciting, yet very foolish. There were no other vehicles on the highway at 3 AM, and I cranked up those wild stallions and drove that roadster at 120 miles an hour. All the streets were totally empty. I figured that if a policeman stopped me, I could tell him that my mother was taking her last breath and dying. I thought that he or she would surely have mercy on me. Fortunately, I did not pass by the doughnut shop on the way, so I did not see any cops. (Just so you know, I have several friends who are law enforcement officers, so I'm just adding a little bit of doughnut humor at their expense.) If Carol had been with me, she would have had a heart attack or dug her claws into my right forearm and would have been justified in doing so. It was a great time to feel the need for speed.

Carol and I both enjoy our muscle cars, and we have made friends with other SSR fanatics around the country. We often attend SSR events where different people show off their collector's items, and it is great fun. It's nice to be around nuts like us who share our passion for this amazing truck.

As you know, I lost both of my daughters in the accident. I am fortunate to have a wonderful stepson whose name is Dave. He is tall, dark, and handsome with green eyes and brown hair. When he was very young, he played ice hockey up until the time he finished high school. He also has an amazing work ethic, having worked all the way through high school. He is a graduate from Columbine High School. (Yes, where the infamous shootings took place in 1999.) He is a college graduate from Columbia University with a Bachelor of Science in computer science. For a college project, Dave and four other classmates designed a computer program. Dave took charge of the project, and the group designed an interface for people like me who are visually impaired. He named this project "Joe." His professor was so impressed with the program that he asked if he could use it in his future classes as a demonstration of the gold standard. As you can tell, I am very proud to have Dave as my stepson. I never had a son, so Dave is a true blessing to me.

Lisa is my stepdaughter by Carol and is currently a student at Columbine High School as well. She is petite, about 5 feet tall, with blonde hair and beautiful blue eyes. Lisa is very artistic and has a gift for creating beautiful paintings. She has always been the one in the family who makes her gifts and does not buy them. We are always glad, because the gifts she makes are always spectacular and amazingly creative. One of my most prized possessions is a coffee mug Lisa made for me. On one side of the white mug, she created an original logo that says "Joe Airways." It looks like a logo for a real airline and has black letters, blue and red shading, and a green airplane. The other side of the mug bears the inscription, "Happy Father's Day Joe, Love Lisa."

I fully expect to go to a famous art museum one day to see her work. Because of her creative mind, she keeps us laughing with her "Lisa-isms." One year we tried to explain daylight savings time to her and told her that we would move the clocks back one hour. She was very concerned with the time change and was convinced that we would all get mixed up and miss church. She was also the one who inspired us to adopt our beloved Rhodesian Ridgeback dog 6 1/2 years ago, and Eris has been an amazing member of our family. They say a dog is man's best friend, and that was so true with Eris.

My stepchildren feel like my true family. We, of course, all have the ups and downs of a biological family, but I truly love Dave and Lisa. I think it's a little more difficult with a blended family, but I definitely think of them as mine. Carol is the disciplinarian of the family, and that makes it easier for me to not be heavy.

Overall, life is very, very good. I have a wonderful wife, wonderful friends, and a wonderful family with two remarkable stepchildren. I have hundreds of great friends all around the United States, and I get to travel for free. I have my health, I have my faith, and I have fun no matter where I go and what I do. For reasons that you now understand, I appreciate life every day. As you read this, I am now embarking on a new journey as a professional speaker and a book author. I believe that I survived for a reason—to share my message with the world in order to help people find purpose in their lives.

As I sat listening to Joe and watching Carol smile at him in the way people who are in love do, I was so happy for them both. The happy ending where the guy gets the girl and a great girl at that. It was great to hear about their sweet courtship and to see Joe grinning ear to ear. Joe is not a lone wolf; he likes to be in a family pack, and he finally has that. It proves that someone can face devastating loss and eventually win and be happy. The movie has a happy ending, and you have to like that. He deserves it. I stretched back in my seat.

"Well, guys, that was great information. Now I know the whole story. I must tell you how delighted I am for your success." I looked at my watch. "I don't want to, but I guess I should be getting you back to the airport."

Joe stood up slowly and wobbled a bit. "Sorry, I get a little stiff when I sit for a long time." I noticed he had gently grabbed Carol's forearm for support.

"I understand… you are, after all, the bionic man with all your pins and screws," I teased.

On the way to the car, Carol provided her shoulder for Joe to use when he needed balance.

I dropped them off at the airport with a mix of hugs and handshakes.

"Let's do a call next week, Joe. We only have one more chapter."

Joe smiled, "Yeah, it's hard to believe. Just e-mail me dates and times you are around."

Endnote

1. Josiah G. Holland, quoted on *Happy Publishing;* http://www.happypublishing.com/blog/marriage-quotes-2/; accessed May 19, 2011.

Chapter 10

Taming the Beast
of Adversity

It is easy enough to be pleasant, when life flows by like a song. But the man worthwhile is the one who can smile, when everything goes dead wrong. For the test of the heart is troubled, and it always comes with the years. And the smiles that is worth the praises of earth is the smile that shines through tears.—Ella Wheeler Wilcox[1]

From my office, I dialed Joe's phone number in Colorado. It rang a few times.

"Hello?" Joe answered.

"Hey, Joe, this is…" I started.

"Oh, hey, Mr. Shawn. How are you?" he interrupted.

"I am doing well, Joe. Boy, can you believe we are on the last chapter? It seems like the time has flown; no pun intended."

"Yep. You're right," sighed Joe.

"So Joe, the reason I wanted to talk today is to interview you for the last chapter. I feel like I know your life inside and out at this point, but I have some questions that I just have to ask. These are the questions that I think readers would want to know."

"Okay, more details about my life?" he asked.

"Well, sort of, but I think that people will most want to know how you were able to overcome such physical, emotional, and mental adversity. See, I think that everyone in their lifetime struggles with all of those things," I explained.

"Sure, Shawn. I can give you my take on the way that I handled it, but I don't know if there's a right or wrong answer when handling adversity," Joe replied.

"Yes, Joe. You're right. But you certainly are someone who has had a lot of practice!" I said chuckling.

"So, what are your thoughts? How do people handle adversity?"

"That, my friend, is a very good question," said Joe, his tone of voice becoming very reflective. "Let me start with some other adversity that I experienced that you don't know about, and then I will provide some general thoughts about how I overcame that kind of adversity."

"Sounds good, Joe," I said as I prepared to listen to the final chapter of Joe's story.

Early in our married days, Carol and I had some devastating financial adversity visit our door. A friend of ours had gotten me into a very successful stock-trading program that was operated by a very successful experienced trader by the name of Corrine McNabb. I had given her some of my blood money to invest and grow. It was going pretty well. Every month I would get a statement showing 5 to 10 percent increases, which were believable as a good trader could do that with protective hedges on both sides of the trade. Keep in mind that this was way before the Bernie Madoff era. I wish that I could say that I invested with her, made a million dollars, and walked away into the sunset. I wish the story had a happier ending, but it doesn't. Not by a long shot.

We received word from the office of the Attorney General in Utah that she was being indicted for running a scam and that our money was lost. Just like that. The state of Utah was able to recover a fair amount of the funds, but they decided to pay back Utah residents first (I think it must have been an election year) and that did not leave anything for out-of-state residents, such as myself and my friends. Wow. It was a shock to my system because the woman had seemed so credible and many friends had great results with her. It was definitely a blow to the middle of my solar plexus and a massive hit on my bank account.

Humor has often been a helpful tool for me in handling adversity. At the time, I chuckled to myself as I thought about a song from the old country television variety show *Hee Haw*. They did a routine where Buck Owens and Roy Clark sang a duet:

> Gloom, despair, and agony on me,
> Deep, dark depression, excessive misery,
> If it weren't for bad luck,
> (Whoaoaoaoaoaoa)
> I'd have no luck at all,
> Gloom, despair, and agony on me.[2]

Of course, while they were singing the song, there was someone in the background letting out a mournful wail after the third line, and it was quite humorous. They did it every week, and it got a laugh every time.

My financial woes were not over. We had also invested with other experienced traders. They were instructors for the Wade Cook trading seminars (which was, at the time, a very famous and supposedly successful organization). The premise to their training was that they would be protected whether the stock went up or down. We were also getting monthly returns from these folks. One day, while I was in Colorado getting outpatient treatment in the hyperbaric chamber, Carol received a call from our attorney friend in Utah. This attorney had introduced us to the traders, Trevor and Linda. When I came out to the car after my treatment, I found Carol in the car waiting for me with tears in her eyes. When I asked her what was wrong, my heart sunk as she told me that Trevor and Linda had entered a trade without protection and had lost the majority of the funds, which was about $700,000.

I was completely and utterly stunned and felt like the wind had been knocked out of me. After all, a great friend had recommended these traders, and we had done careful research to make sure they were legitimate. In fact, before we invested with them, we flew to Salt Lake City for a visit. Their offices were very impressive, and the working space in the office looked like NASA flight control. Each desk had four computers that streamed live stock option data before our eyes. It was an amazing sight to see. There were two large television flat screens on the wall that broadcasted Bloomberg Financial and CNBC. Their office, their expertise, and their background were all very impressive. However, this time the results were not. In 2005, Wade Cook was personally indicted by the federal government for federal tax fraud and owed millions in back taxes. Most people don't realize that investing is risky, and we always assumed that we would get rewards from our investments. But just like Las Vegas, sometimes the odds are not in your favor and you lose. Not every investment is a winner. With most of our money gone, we walked away with about $100,000.

So, I'm sure you're thinking at this point that we put the final $100,000 in a safe, conservative, low yield bank account, but that is not what we did. Remember when Oliver would say to Hardy, "Here's another fine mess you've gotten us into!"? Well, the $100,000 was enough to get us into a large real estate project during the Florida real estate boom. A friend of ours, Brian, who lived on our ski lake, had made a fortune developing raw land and selling it to developers so that they could build communities. According to Brian, his net worth was close to $100 million.

Instead of being named Brian, his name should have been Midas, because he seemed to have the Midas golden touch. Brian found some land (about 5,700 acres) in central Florida right along Interstate 75 that would make an excellent community. He had an architect draw out the subdivision. The plans were beautiful, and I had a feeling that it would do well. After all, Florida real estate was on the rise, and we could get a very nice return on our investment. Out of 45 investors, we invested the smallest amount. Our $100,000 was combined with $150,000 from the seller, who financed us so that we could meet the $250,000 minimum investment requirement. We had small potatoes in the entire deal. We knew that Brian had invested $12 million, so he had a lot more to lose than us.

As the market rose, Brian received an offer from a buyer that would have doubled our return. Everyone in the group agreed that Brian would make all the decisions, because he had so much experience and success in the industry. He made a pass on that offer as he felt that market conditions would continue to rise. Everyone reading this knows what happened. The economy suddenly fell, and the real estate bubble burst in a flash. In Florida, it exploded. The potential buyer was, of course, long gone by then. We were all paying on a note for land that was not selling. Of course, no land in this area of Florida was selling at that time.

It became a total loss and Brian had to give the land back to the person whom he had purchased it from. Ironically, we could have doubled our money early on and looked for another deal. Brian's past successes made him overconfident, and I believe that he lost his ability to be objective. The loss on our part was our entire investment, but Brian's loss was huge. In the blink of an eye, he lost close to $20 million. That is a lot of money no matter where you're from. Brian's downhill spiral took us with him. This was the last $100,000 of my settlement from the accident. With this loss, like so many other people, we became a paycheck to paycheck family.

I did have one golden nest egg left. I had bought a one-acre lot on the ski lake (the same lake Kelley and I had built our home on) from my good friend, Art Marino. I had intended to build my next home on it with a new family someday. We needed to sell that lot to get out of some debt. We actually sold it at the peak of the bubble and nearly tripled my investment. That paid off our small Florida home and allowed us to buy a nicer home in Littleton, Colorado. The Colorado home has a lot of space for entertaining, which we love to do. We love having large parties and dinners with our many friends. We even hosted a political promotion party for a senator and a hopeful congressman with about 75 people. When 75 people fit into your home comfortably (and you don't have to worry about who took a shower that day) then you are in pretty good shape.

After the boat company sank and we lost our investments because of those fine expert stock traders, we went to see a bankruptcy attorney. Fortunately, I was still getting my disability checks without fail every month, so we were able to get by without going bankrupt. But we were on the edge of the bankruptcy cliff, and our toes were hanging over the edge. We have a small mortgage on the Colorado home, and the Florida home is free and clear, which is a nice feeling. I did have to sell the beautiful home on the lake that Kelley and I built. Carol and I bought a smaller home in West Palm. That was our saving grace in order to reduce our debt. I have learned that the best things in life are not things, and this is now the financial philosophy that I embrace.

Once in a lifetime, you may be fortunate enough to have a pet that is the most incredible pet ever born. We were given that once-in-a-lifetime animal—a dog named Eris. She was a large, 110-pound Rhodesian Ridgeback with a beautiful, short-haired wheaten coat and big brown eyes. Perhaps her best physical feature was a set of the longest, floppiest ears a dog can have. Eris slept at the foot of our bed, and every morning about 6 A.M. she would wake up and flap those ears as loud as she could. It was the best alarm clock I ever had. Her face was very expressive with dark markings around her eyes and on her nose. When she was puzzled, confused, or hungry, she would wrinkle her forehead up to let you know something was not right.

All the books say that Ridgebacks are extremely intelligent. Eris wasn't the brightest dog, but what she lacked in brains, she made up for in her unconditional love and loyalty. She was actually like the best child you could ever dream of. She was the happiest dog on the planet and her antics kept us laughing nonstop. She was very klutzy and was constantly bonking her head as she came into contact with a wall, a table, or us. When we got her, she was about three years old and had already been given the name Eris. Eris, in case you do not know, was the Greek goddess of strife and discord. Our Eris was just the opposite; she was the goddess of love and loyalty. She licked the battle scars on my feet and knees in an attempt to heal me with her magic, healing tongue. That was awesome that she tried to heal my once badly broken body, and we lovingly nicknamed her "Doctor Eris."

About a month before her tenth birthday, Eris' health began to deteriorate, and we had to make a gut-wrenching decision. Some of her organs were beginning to fail, and we knew we had to end her suffering. We picked November 24, 2010, the day before Thanksgiving. The night before Eris was to be put to sleep, our daughter, Lisa, was so upset that she slept on the floor by the dog all night long with her arms wrapped around the beloved hound that she had adored since she was a little kid. We knew that Eris was suffering, and it was the humane thing to do, but it tore all of us up. Our family must have cried a million tears in the weeks that followed Eris' death. We all knew that there would never be another Eris, as she was a one-of-a-kind dog.

As traumatic as it was to lose Eris, there is no comparison between losing your beloved hound and losing your wife and children. It is nowhere close to that kind of heartache. Believe it or not, many people have told me that they know how I feel, only to go on to tell me that they just lost a pet. I know that they are trying to be kind and empathetic, but when you compare the loss of a pet to the loss of a family member or, as in my case a whole family, it makes my skin crawl. I don't dismiss their loss, and I know it was painful for them. I have been there too, but it is ludicrous for them to think that they have the same kind of heartache. If you are ever comforting someone who has lost a member of their family, just tell them you're sorry and ask how you can help them. Please don't say, "I know how you feel," or compare any of your losses to theirs.

People often ask me how I am able to live with such adversity and overcome my emotional, physical, and financial losses. Let me address each one of these individually.

In dealing with the emotional loss of my family, the grief was initially brutal when I was alone, and the sorrow would hit me like a big whirlwind. I will tell you that the girls are always in my heart. As time progressed, my sorrow became less and less over time. There is a popular saying out there that "time heals all wounds." I believe that saying should be rewritten to be more accurate; it should say, "God heals in time." When you lose your wife and two beautiful daughters in an awful instant, it leaves a humongous hole to heal. Without God's help, I could not have gotten through the devastating loss. As time passes, my girls are always in my thoughts, but the pain itself has been healed.

The healing process is different for everyone, and some people take much longer to heal. Since my personality is a positive one, it was easier for me to get past the sorrow as that is a negative. I drove through the negatives to reach the positives, so that I could bring happiness and joy back to my life. I was fortunate that I was raised in a family that helped me form a positive personality. My other secret weapon for dealing with the emotional loss was the amazing support of family and friends. My sister Rose, who moved in with me to take care of me, is also a very positive person and a female version of Tigger. She is always happy, and her happiness is infectious. My other siblings are also positive.

I have so many friends that I cannot mention them individually, but they were always there for me, even if it was just taking me to lunch or a ride on a motorcycle, having me over for dinner, or just being a friend. I had wise friends who were there for me when I needed to talk or needed counsel. Consequently, I never felt a need to seek out therapy or treatment psychologically and was able to overcome it with my own strength and my friends. The amazing love of those friends and family was a gift of love that still warms the fires of my heart.

People also ask me how I maintained a positive attitude, despite all that I have experienced. That is a silly question, because remember, I am Tigger! In all seriousness, there are sad times that come and go, but I do not dwell on them for long periods. We can all learn from the wise philosopher, Tigger, that life does have peaks and valleys. But if we remain hopeful and positive, the valleys will start to rise upward, and we will eventually reach another peak. I bet you did not know that Tigger said that.

Some people also think that I deserve to carry some bitterness based on what has happened. I don't. I do not worry about people who are mean to me. They, for some reason, do not have peace in their hearts. They also do not want me to have peace in my heart and, for some reason, are trying to get to me. I just try to forgive them and move on, because otherwise, I have allowed them to win. They will not win. It is human nature to be upset and bitter when bad things do happen. It would be easy for me to become bitter and wallow in my own self-pity.

When we have sadness in our lives, it is hard to look at a glass as half full instead of half empty, because all of the good stuff seems to be gone. It is easy to look at the sky as being partly cloudy instead of partly clear. The key is to find joy that helps outweigh the sadness and bitterness. So every person has a choice between either being bitter and pessimistic or happy and optimistic. As for me, I choose the latter. When I hear people complain that they have a good reason to complain (because maybe something in their life is not going well), I try to show them mercy. If someone complains all of the time about little things, then I try to always point out another view that is more positive.

I think one of the keys for me in handling my physical loss and injury is to not dwell on what I *used* to have, but on what *I have now*. Sure, it would be great to get into a time machine like Michael J. Fox did in *Back to the Future,* but that's not going to happen. As a side note, I am sure Michael J. Fox would probably like to jump in the machine, too, because of his struggle with Parkinson's. This has become the *new normal* for me. I willingly accept the cards that I have been dealt, but I'm always looking to improve my hand.

At times, it may seem as if you have a hand of bad cards, but don't give up looking for aces, because you may end up with kings and queens. I am diligent in improving my physical impairment, and I never give up. Ever. Having a new normal does not preclude me from giving my best to whatever I can do. Yes, I know I was once very athletic and able to excel at sports like skiing. That is true. I was once a heck of an athletic specimen. I do not consider myself as disabled or handicapped, but as physically challenged instead. Now I am grateful to be walking at all, even though it is a wobble of a walk!

As far as financial adversity, I really am grateful that I worked for a good company that had an amazing disability plan. This was, of course, not luck, because I had worked hard to get such a great job flying for a major airline. I am fortunate to have a stable income even though I do stumble into a financial sinkhole every now and then. (Don't we all?) Would it be best to not have had the financial losses that I had? Of course. But when financial losses do come, the only positive choice is to pick up what pieces are left and move on. In my mind, it's really the only choice that you have. Losing money also gives you a unique perspective, because when money is gone for good with no chance of recovery, you start to be grateful just for the shirt on your back! You appreciate the small things. I really feel for families and people who may lose their jobs due to the economy or to health issues. They are not fortunate enough to be part of a disability program. Some people even end up on the street or are homeless when a financial hammer comes down on them in the job market, and it is difficult to replace what they had. I don't concentrate on what I had; I concentrate on what I have.

Sometimes people ask me why this all happened to me. The answer is, I don't know. Bad things happen to people almost every day all over the globe. It doesn't have to be an airplane crash. There are many other things like hurricanes, floods, and other natural disasters. It might be something as silly as falling off of a ladder. As M. Scott Peck said in his famous book, *The Road Less Traveled*, "Life is unfair." That is the opening sentence of the book, and he says to the readers that they will be happier if they understand that concept.[3] It is true; life can be unfair to many people, and it may bring on bad things. Bad things do happen to good people all of the time, because it is, after all, not a perfect world.

In my situation, as you know, I tried to get back to the runway with a severely crippled airplane, and I almost made it. Obviously, I thought that was the best option at the time. The engine was continually losing power as the spark plugs fouled out due to too much fuel and not enough air. It was a bad part that failed on the engine, and I am sure that if the mechanic could go back in time, he would have put on a better part that would have had less chance of failing. He could not have felt good about what happened.

I do not believe, nor will I ever believe, that there was some higher power saying it was time for Joe to lose his family and his health. I wasn't specially selected for this honor. I don't believe it was written in the book of fate on the day that I was born or that it was "predestined" to happen. It was an accident. Some people have even said to me that "There is always a reason," or "Everything happens for a reason." Yes, there was a reason— *the engine quit on me!* There is no other reason. Do they think there was another reason that my wife, daughters, and health were taken from me? Was I being taught some lesson? Was I being punished for some reason? It boggles my mind. Accidents don't have reason and logic; that is why they happened. So don't try and justify a reason. It is like trying to justify why some knucklehead walks into a convenience store and wins the lotto for $123 million. It can't be explained.

What happened was horrific, and it happened to me. Thankfully, I have survived to share my story so that many other people who face other kinds of adversity in their lives may find some comfort or inspiration. I would love to help them get through their adversity and beyond to a place where there is less pain and suffering. Here is my key message that I want to bring to the world:

> It may look grim at first, but with the right attitude, you
> can find happiness and joy again!

You really can. Many accident victims and soldiers who are paralyzed or have missing limbs have to deal with a whole *new normal*. They have to learn how to do new things with challenges they never dreamed of having, which can be a nightmare. But they eventually accept it.

When I was first injured, I knew that I would be back someday doing the things I used to do before, and I knew I would be going back to the cockpit and flying planes. No matter what the challenge was, I have thought this way my whole life. Getting back to normal meant that I had to work hard for it. Even though medical professionals said that I would never walk again, I knew that I would. Doctors are not gods; they are people who happen to go to medical school. They are smart people, but they are still people who have flaws like all of us. They have opinions, which are sometimes right. But, guess what. Sometimes they are wrong and they underestimate. They do not understand what a Tigger can do!

I was going to go for the gold, and I was going to retrain myself to walk. Remember, I was a father who helped Laura and Tara take their first steps. So, I knew it was not immediate and took many trials to get there. They fell down a lot, landing on their cushy diapers on their behinds. They would try to walk by holding onto the coffee table. They held on and walked around it, and they learned. I am happy that I was home when they both took their first steps, as I would stand them up and have them walk toward me as I backed up. I encouraged them to keep going. Those were great lessons that I learned from my little angels about walking.

As hard as I worked for it, my body healed tremendously, but not ever completely. As time passed, I realized that my injuries were greater than I thought. I still envision further healing and improvement. I still believe that. I am taking baby steps, but they are small; some people don't even see them, but they are still steps. I love the movie *What About Bob* with Bill Murray and Richard Dreyfuss. In the movie, Bob is a patient of the psychiatrist, played by Richard Dreyfuss. He tells Bob that he "must take baby steps to improve. It is one baby step after another and keeping the baby steps going to get you where they add up to big steps." That is what I was doing—and what I am doing today.

I do know now that I have impairments that may be with me forever, but I never give up hope. Hope is the positive expectation of a fulfilled future.

We have great bodies that can heal, but I feel that it takes positive motivation to feed our brains in order to keep improving. I am grateful for my abilities now, and I work out at the gym to keep getting stronger, because if I give up on myself, I better learn to love a wheelchair because that's where I would end up. If keeping my body strong will prevent that, then that becomes my job. So I tell myself in the morning, "Joe, it's a new day, and it is time to get up and at 'em!" I go to the gym in the morning so that I can go home, shower, and continue the rest of my day with positive energy. It is important for me not to let the "lazy bone" mentality ever set in as it is very important to start each day with a positive outlook.

From early childhood, I learned to never give up, and I was always motivated to press on. That is how I became successful at my flying career. I kept improving, and that's what got me to the next level in my career. If you have a goal to work toward, keep your focus, work hard, and you can achieve it.

If you have friends who are going through adversity, just be a supportive friend, because you cannot feel their stress and pressure. They are going through a valley of hurt and pain, and the strength of their support system will determine how quickly they can climb out of the valley. As a friend, you should be a comfort, to help them climb out of the valley. Adversity could look like having a disability, being in a wheelchair, suffering financial devastation, or losing a loved one. Like the song that was played at my wedding, *All You Need is Love*. The people around you who are going through adversity need your love and support. I know it sounds like some cheesy dime store greeting card, but all I can tell you is it worked for me. I live the redeeming power of love.

The other mindset that has helped me greatly through my adversity is to find my joy. I know that sounds like something from a kooky motivational seminar, but it is true. The more time I spent doing things that brought me joy, the faster I healed emotionally and physically. I love spending quality time with family and good friends. I love traveling anywhere. To me, traveling is always a joyful adventure even if I have been there before. I know that I'm going to see and do something different, or even repeat something that was fun last time. I just love adventures. So connect to your joy, because life can end in the blink of an eye, twisting you upside down and inside out. Don't wait to do the things that bring you joy. Love and live your life to the fullest.

I also love humor, and it is a tool for healing both my heart and soul. I love listening to comedy CDs or funny routines on movies and on television. As the old saying goes, laughter truly is the best medicine. It helps cheer you up and puts a smile on your face. When I was in the hospital for such a long time, I had friends bring me the tapes of Abbott and Costello in order to lighten my day. In fact, I found out recently that laughter actually does have a medicinal impact. When people laugh, a whole bunch of hormones are released that are natural "uppers." I somehow already knew that.

Sometimes, when I am flying on a plane, I strike up a conversation with the person next to me. Once I have told them my story, they are surprised that I still like to fly. Well, I know how well the pilots are trained. They have to pass simulator check rides every six months. The mechanical and maintenance work on planes is also highly regulated, and any mechanical issues with commercial aircraft are repaired before leaving. There are checks and double checks. Besides, flying is still a passion for me, even though I had an engine failure in a single engine aircraft with horrific results. I still miss flying as the pilot. If my vision ever heals enough to fly, then you'll find me happily back in the cockpit seat because flying is in my blood.

We all have some form of adversity that comes and goes in our lives. Some people have more than others. Some challenges may be easy, and some challenges may be difficult. My mission is to share my story of overcoming some of the most horrific adversity ever to show others that they can overcome theirs. It may look grim, but if you are still breathing, then there is still life left to live. It doesn't matter if your life after adversity is lived from a wheelchair or while running a marathon. I want to help people live their lives to the fullest and help them realize their full potential.

That is why I have now embraced a new career as an author and a professional motivational speaker. I plan to travel the country speaking to groups, associations, and companies to show them they can overcome adversity. If *I* can do it, I know that *they* can do it also. It is a message that needs to be shared amongst all the doom and gloom of today's world. Have you ever seen the evening news? I guess the sky really is falling!

So I want to share this message with people to help them live better lives. I think that Marianne Williamson may have said what I am trying to say in a more eloquent fashion:

> Our deepest fear is not that we are inadequate. Our deepest fear is that we are powerful beyond measure. It is our light not our darkness that most frightens us. Your playing small does not serve the world. There is nothing enlightened about shrinking so that other people won't feel

insecure around you. We are all meant to shine as children do. It's not just in some of us, it is in everyone. And as we let our own light shine we unconsciously give other people permission to do the same. As we are liberated from our own fear our presence automatically liberates others.[4]

Our memories of yesterday are the things that give us courage to face tomorrow!

Thank you for reading the story of my horrific accident and my triumph.

My name is Joe Townsend, and I am *The Soul SURVIVOR!*

ENDNOTES

1. Ella Wheeler Wilcox, quoted on *Quote Lady;* http://www.quotelady. com/authors/author-w.html; accessed May 19, 2011.

2. Buck Owens and Roy Clark, "Gloom, Despair, and Agony on Me," *Hee Haw* TV show (1969-1992); http://lyricsplayground.com/alpha/ songs/g/gloomdespairandagonyonme.shtml; accessed May 19, 2011.

3. M. Scott Peck, *The Road Less Traveled* (New York: Touchstone Publishers, 2003), 15.

4. This is often erroneously attributed to the inaugural address of Nelson Mandela. The quote is actually from Marianne Williamson, *A Return to Love: Reflections on the Principles of "A Course in Miracles"* (New York: Harper Collins, 1992), Chapter 7, Section 3.

About the Authors

Joe Townsend

Joe was born in Winston-Salem, North Carolina, and grew up in Florida. At age 14, Joe joined the Civil Air Patrol, and at 17 he worked as a ramp agent, handling baggage for United and National Airlines. As a ramp agent, Joe cleaned the interior of airplanes, caught his first glimpse of a cockpit, and brushed shoulders with pilots. Soon after, he enrolled in Palm Beach Junior College and pursued a career in aviation. He eventually graduated from Emery-Riddle Aeronautical University and became a pilot.

Joe's flying career has allowed him to work as a pilot for a private jet charter company as well as fly for a commercial airline. He has enjoyed flying many famous clients including Tammy Wynette, Brenda Lee, Jack Nicklaus, Lady Bird Johnson, Arthur Ashe, John Glenn, Jerry Reed, and his favorite, Jimmy Buffett!

He married his long-time sweetheart Kelley in 1985, and they had two daughters, Laura Lee and Tara Nicole. In 1996, Joe was flying with his family when their aircraft developed a mechanical problem and crashed. Joe was the soul survivor! His injuries were so severe that his life took a dramatic twist, and he has been on long-term medical disability since.

Fortunately, Joe has been happily married to his new wife Carol since September 2001.

Shawn Doyle

Shawn Doyle is the President of New Light Learning and Development Inc., a leadership, motivation, and sales effectiveness company.

Shawn has a passion for human development. He has an avid belief in lifelong learning.

For the last 22 years, Shawn has developed and implemented training programs on sales, communication, and leadership. Shawn's clients include Charter Media, Insight Media, Kraft, IBM, Smith Barney, Microsoft, Wyeth, and the Los Alamos National Defense Laboratory. He won the coveted Pinnacle Award for outstanding leadership and has earned the distinction of Advanced Toastmaster Bronze from Toastmaster's International. He has had articles published in *Training and Development Magazine, Creative Training Techniques,* and *Miller-Heiman's Best Few.* Shawn has also authored ten books.

Shawn lives in Pennsylvania with his wife of many years and their collection of amazing cats.

OTHER BOOKS BY SHAWN DOYLE

The Ten Foundations of Motivation

The Manager's Pocket Guide to Motivating Employees

The Manager's Pocket Guide to Training

Juiced! How to Get Creative and Stay Creative
co-authored with David Newman

Sales Science
co-authored with David Newman

Wired! How to Get and Stay Creative in the World of Cable

Two Months to Motivation

Cartoon Magic—Easy Object Anyone Can Draw

The 6 Essentials for Success in Business and Life
co-authored with several authors

Dr. Babb's Idea Lab

In the right hands, This Book will Change Lives!

Most of the people who need this message will not be looking for this book. To change their lives, you need to put a copy of this book in their hands.

> *But others (seeds) fell into good ground, and brought forth fruit, some a hundred-fold, some sixty-fold, some thirty-fold* (Matthew 13:8).

Our ministry is constantly seeking methods to find the good ground, the people who need this anointed message to change their lives. Will you help us reach these people?

> *Remember this—a farmer who plants only a few seeds will get a small crop. But the one who plants generously will get a generous crop* (2 Corinthians 9:6).

EXTEND THIS MINISTRY BY SOWING
3 BOOKS, 5 BOOKS, 10 BOOKS, OR MORE TODAY,
AND BECOME A LIFE CHANGER!

Thank you,

Don Nori Sr., Founder
Destiny Image
Since 1982